MW01152070

six decades of the Fender telecaster

Muddy Waters and trusty Telecaster

six decades of the Fender® telecaster

THE STORY OF THE WORLD'S FIRST SOLIDBODY ELECTRIC GUITAR

TONY BACON

SIX DECADES OF THE FENDER TELECASTER

Tony Bacon

A BACKBEAT BOOK
First edition 2005
Published by Backbeat Books
600 Harrison Street
San Francisco
CA 94107, US
www.backbeatbooks.com

An imprint of The Music Player Network CMP Media LLC

Devised and published for Backbeat Books by Outline Press Ltd,
2A Union Court, 20-22 Union Road, London SW4 6JP, England
www.backbeatuk.com

ISBN 0-87930-856-7
ISBN13/EAN 978-0879-30856-8

Text copyright © Tony Bacon. Volume copyright © 2005 Backbeat UK.
All rights reserved. No part of this book covered by the copyrights hereon may be reproduced or copied in any manner whatsoever without written permission, except in the case of brief quotations embodied in articles or reviews where the source should be made clear. For more information contact the publisher.

EDITOR: Simon Smith
DESIGN: Paul Cooper Design
ART DIRECTOR: Nigel Osborne

Origination and print by Colorprint (Hong Kong)

05 06 07 08 09 5 4 3 2 1

contents

Introduction

It's the oldest solidbody electric guitar still going strong – which is not surprising when you consider the fact that it was the very first. Way back in 1950, before anyone had even thought of rock'n'roll, Fender came up with the first commercially marketed solidbody electric. Uncluttered and straightforward it may have been, but those are the attributes that remain at the heart of the Telecaster's appeal.

So what is it about the Tele? It's a simple, honest, playable guitar. But most of all it comes down to that sound. You usually have to work at a Tele to make it do what you want, but the classic single-coil instrument has a dry bite and a twangy, cutting punch that the best players relish. And now the humbucker'd Teles are back in fashion, there's a different kind of kick there too if you want it.

I've interviewed dozens of Fender players and Fender people to illustrate this story of the Telecaster through its six decades of development. It's a constant source of delight and wonder to see Teles turning up in all manner of new music, and of course it's always a joy to revisit the great music that defined the guitar as a modern classic. As James Burton told me: "In studios they'll say oh, you've got to have this guitar and that guitar. And I say why do I need all those guitars? It's right here. Know what I'm saying?"[1]

I like to think of the Telecaster as a grown-up guitar. It's a magnet for anyone who's been through all the gimmickry and gadgetry of the latest wonder-guitar. If you haven't already succumbed, you're sure to come to appreciate the elegant, unpretentious simplicity of this instrument, one that effortlessly reflects the character and the will of the player in charge.

"If there were no Telecasters," said Jeff Buckley, "there would be no James Brown, no Zeppelin *I*, *II* and *III*, no Elvis, no country, and no Prince."[2] So there it is. There's the body, there's the neck. There are the pickups and there are the knobs. Nothing more, nothing less. Now off you go and make it your own. You're in good company.

***Tony Bacon**, Bristol, England, September 2005*

Jonny Greenwood of Radiohead leans into his Tele, onstage in 2003

Fender's new solidbody electric guitar was finally put on sale to musicians as the Telecaster in April 1951 following months of testing and tweaking and trouble for Leo Fender and his team. The instrument had debuted the previous year, first as the Esquire and then the Broadcaster. Leo's small firm was already turning out electric lap-steel guitars and amplifiers in a couple of buildings in Fullerton, Orange County, but soon the Telecaster's simple playability would lead to unimagined success and fortune.

All this was a long way from the Fender family's humble beginnings. Clarence Leonidas Fender was born in 1909, in a barn near the Anaheim/Fullerton border in the Los Angeles area. He would come to consider Fullerton as his home town. Leo's parents ran a 'truck farm', growing vegetables and fruit for the market – including the area's famous oranges. The Fenders had put up the barn first before they could afford to build a house. Leo's father had come to California from Illinois, and Leo's ancestors were American right back to his great-great-great-great grandfather, who had come to the United States from Auerbach in Germany.

Leo's second wife talked about a revealing episode from his early years. "When he was a little boy his father told him that the only thing worthwhile in this whole world was what you accomplished at work, and that if you were not working you were lazy, which was a sin. So Leo judged himself and everyone else by that – and himself hardest of all."[3]

Leo worked in the accounts section of the state highway department and then a tyre distribution company, but his hobby was always electronics. In his 20s he built amplifiers and PA systems for public events such as sports gatherings and dances. He took a few piano lessons before trying the saxophone, but was never serious, and never learned to play the guitar.

When he lost his accounts job in the depression he took the bold step of opening his own radio and record store in Fullerton. This happened around the end of the 1930s. The Fender Radio Service, as he called the new retail and repair shop, seemed a natural step for the ambitious, newly-married 30-year-old. Leo advertised his wares and services on his business card as "electrical appliances, phonograph records, musical instruments & repairs, public address systems, sheet music". The new store on South Spadra brought introductions to many local musicians and to characters in the music and electronics businesses, and during the first few years Leo met several people who would prove important to his future success. First was a professional violinist and lap-steel guitarist, Clayton Orr Kauffman, known to all simply as Doc.

The story goes that some time around 1940 Doc brought an amp into Leo's shop for repair and the two got chatting.

Doc had amplified his own guitars and worked on designs for an electric guitar and a vibrato-arm. By this time Leo had already begun to look into the potential for electric guitars and to play around with pickup designs. A crude solidbody guitar that Fender and Kauffman built in 1943 purely to test these early pickups – one design for which was patented in '44 – is today in Roy Acuff's museum at Opryland, Nashville.

Doc went to work for an aircraft company during World War II, but the two incorrigible tinkerers still found time to get together and to come up with a design for a record-changer good enough to net them $5,000. Some of this money went into bolstering their shortlived company, K&F (for Kauffman & Fender). They began proper production of electric lap-steel guitars and small amplifiers in November 1945.

Lap-steel guitar playing, often called Hawaiian guitar, had been fashionable in America since the 1920s and was still tremendously popular. The steel had been the first type of guitar to go electric in the 1930s. Several innovative companies, with Rickenbacker in the lead, experimented with electro-magnetic pickups, fixing them to guitars and connecting them to small amplifiers.

The steel had become popular as an easy-to-play instrument suitable for beginners, but the electric version had also proved enormously appealing among professional musicians, especially in Hawaiian music and in country and western bands. The steel guitar was played on the lap or mounted on legs. The name came not from its construction – Fender's steels were all wooden – but from the metal bar used in the player's left hand to stop the raised strings, which were generally tuned to an open chord. During the 1930s and later the term 'Spanish' was used to identify the other (then less popular) type of guitar that was played upright against the body. Leo called this the 'standard' guitar.

"ELECTRICAL APPLIANCES, PHONOGRAPH RECORDS, MUSICAL INSTRUMENTS & REPAIRS, PUBLIC ADDRESS SYSTEMS, SHEET MUSIC."

An early Fender Radio Store business card itemises the services that Leo offered

Doc Kauffman wrote later about the early days of K&F. "[Leo and I] would go down to the store, and at the rear was a metal building that housed the guitar department, and we would work till midnight." This description of a "guitar department" is certainly optimistic. Most people who saw the "metal building" have described it as a tin shack hastily and cheaply assembled behind Leo's radio store. Doc continued his account: "I used to assemble all our instruments and string them up and play a few steel licks, and Leo used to say he could tell how production was coming along by counting the tunes I was playing."[4]

Another significant person Leo started working with at this early stage was Don Randall, who as we shall see would become a key contributor to the later success of the Fender company. Randall was general manager of Radio & Television Equipment Co (known as Radio-Tel), based in Santa Ana, some 15 miles south of Fullerton. Radio-Tel, owned by Francis Hall, became the exclusive distributor of K&F products early in 1946, with salesman Charlie Hayes heading the push to persuade dealers to stock Fender products. One of Randall's customers was the Fender Radio Service.

Leo had not served in World War II, because of a childhood illness that cost him his right eye. Randall, who spent three years in the army, recalled that Leo was able to expand his shop's trade in the war years. "During that period there weren't too many people about to do that kind of business," explained Randall. "When I got out of the service I came back and started doing business with Leo again, selling parts and equipment."[5]

It was around this time that Leo and Doc Kauffman decided to split. "It seems Doc was afraid to carry on with the business," Randall said. Leo was happy to work into the middle of the night at the tin shack making the K&F lap-steel guitars and amps, but apparently Doc wasn't so keen to spend long hours locked away from the world.

Leo recalled the circumstances later: "It cost a lot of money to get into large-scale production, and the 1930s depression was still fresh in Kauffman's mind, so he didn't want to get involved. He had a ranch or farm ... and he was afraid if we got over-extended on credit he might lose it. He thought he'd better pull out while he had a full skin, so in February of '46 he left it all with me."[6]

According to one colleague, Doc – who remained lifelong friends with Leo – was asked later if he resented selling out, given the subsequent success of Fender. "And Doc said no, he was never sore – because Leo would have killed him before he got through with it anyway," referring to the long hours. "Doc liked to spend time with his family. He didn't like staying down the shack till 10 or 11 at night, seven days a week. Anyone that worked with Leo really did have a hard time not over-working, because Leo expected you to be on call all hours."[7]

So Leo and Doc parted. "His worry was right," Leo said later. "We had quite a few hard years ahead."[8] In 1946 Leo called his revised operation Fender Manufacturing, renaming it the Fender Electric Instrument Co in December 1947. He continued to make lap-steels and amps as he had with K&F, but gradually developed new products. He also expanded into larger premises on nearby Pomona Avenue in Fullerton, at the corner of Santa Fe Avenue, separate from the radio store. The new property was described by one observer as "two plain steel buildings, not very handsome". Another Fender associate remembered that the Pomona buildings did not have their own toilets. Consequently, Fender workers had to cross the nearby railroad tracks to use the rest-rooms in the Santa Fe station. Eventually one rather elderly employee couldn't make the treacherous trans-railroad journey, and the next day Leo had no choice but to hire a portable toilet.

DURING THE EARLY YEARS FENDER CAME CLOSE TO FAILING, BUT LEO'S DETERMINATION HELPED PULL THROUGH DIFFICULT TIMES

Dale Hyatt was another important new member of the gradually growing Fender team. He joined the company in January 1946 and would later become a crucial member of the Fender sales team. But one of his early tasks, in late 1947 or early 1948, was to take over the radio store business, because Leo was trying to get things started at Pomona Avenue. However, business was slow and Fender had to rely on a loan from Radio-Tel's Francis Hall to keep going.

Leo was an introverted, hard-working man, prone to long hours and selfless application to the task in hand, happiest when by himself and drawing up designs for new projects. He thought that if there was a product on the market already, he could make it better and cheaper – and make a profit in the process. Despite spectacular later successes, during the early years the new Fender company came perilously close to failing. It was Leo's sheer determination combined with his luck in surrounding himself with clever, dedicated people that would help pull through these difficult times.

Fender guitars: "greater brilliance and presence"

Now that the war was over, there was a general feeling that a fresh start was possible, and one of the processes that many American businessmen began to exploit was mass production. Leo's particular application of this technique to guitar manufacturing was to be his master-stroke, but in these early days he still needed outside expertise in the mass-production of parts. And so another piece of the jigsaw came into place.

Karl Olmsted and his partner Lymon Race left the services in 1947 and decided to start a much-needed tool-and-die company in Fullerton, making specialist tools and dies that customers could use to stamp out metal parts on punch presses. "We were looking for work," Olmsted said, "and Leo had reached the point where he needed dies to be made for production work. They'd been making parts by hand, cutting out the metal any way they could. But he was getting to the point where they wanted to make several of each thing." Race & Olmsted continued to make Fender's tooling and most metal parts for the next 30 years and more. "As it progressed, so we progressed to more complicated, sophisticated, high-production tooling," said Olmsted.[9]

Next to join Fender's company was George Fullerton, who was to become what one colleague described as "Leo's faithful workhorse". The two had met at one of the outdoor events for which Leo was still supplying PA systems, and the young George – who was "going to school, playing music, repairing radios, and delivering furniture" – started to help Leo with the PA events. Gradually, George's radio repair turned to fixing amps and lap-steels, and he began working at Pomona Avenue in February 1948. "It was only a small place then," he remembered, "only two or three people, a couple of girls."[10]

Not only small, but still precarious. Lack of cash-flow was an almost ever-present problem at Fender in those early days. One employee reports that there were times when it was hard to cash Fender cheques in Fullerton – especially if Leo's first wife, Esther, was late in receiving her wages from the phone company. A very early ad for the new Fender company's wares in 1947 showed just three lap-steel guitars and a couple of amplifiers. Fender stressed the plus points of the guitars: "Exclusive new patented pickup unit ... affording greater brilliance and presence. Equal volume output from all strings without compensating adjustments."

Leo and Randall were two highly motivated men with very different ways of working. "Leo sometimes was very resistant to change: you had to prove everything to him," said Dale Hyatt. "Nothing wrong with that, you just had to do it. Randall of course was much the same way. He was also rather stubborn in his realm of thinking. It's been said that they fought like cats and dogs, but I don't believe that's true at all. They couldn't fight – because they just didn't talk to each other, period. But I think one was as good as the other – and they were good for each other. I don't say that Leo Fender was the greatest thing that ever happened to Don Randall or vice versa. No, I think they were the greatest thing that happened to each other."[11]

Leo was certainly single-minded. He would have been happy if he could just continue to slave away in his workshop, sketching out pickup designs or fiddling with a new piece of machinery. As far as he was concerned, the fewer people who got in the way of all this, the better. And generally speaking, Leo was – according to Leo – the only one able to get such things done.

One of his colleagues said: "Leo might come in one morning and buddy, he had something in his mind that he wanted to try. The place is burning down? Let it burn down. He wanted to do what he was on. And he wasn't one to give any compliments. You could tell Leo something and you'd give him an idea. You could tell he was looking straight at you and thinking. Wouldn't say a thing, wouldn't agree that you'd even told him anything. Then later on your idea would show up on something."[12]

Randall wanted a good product at a competitive price that would rock the market, and he often had to shake things up at the factory to get results. Leo, meanwhile, would be changing a particular wiring set-up for the seventh time. He was constantly trying to perfect this guitar or that amp. "Leo was a strange man in a way," Randall said. "He had a fetish for machinery. Nothing was done economically, necessarily. If you could do it on a big machine, let's buy the big machine and use it – when you might have been able to buy the part the machine made a lot cheaper from a supplier."[13]

Karl Olmsted agreed. "Leo would say that he'd like a certain part, and we'd take it back to our workshop. Then I'd say Leo, we'd have to hand-make every one of these, there's no way you can mass-produce it, it's going to be slow and expensive. He would say well, what can you come up with that's cheap and that will make me happy? Almost every job was that way."[14]

Fender's electric lap-steels began to enjoy local and increasingly wider success, on the West Coast and in the Southwest – and increasingly eastwards. The local Fullerton paper reported in November 1949 that the Fender firm was "well known throughout the country" and yet "almost anonymous" in its home town.[15] Then Leo began to think about producing an electric 'Spanish' guitar, in other words one of standard shape and playing style rather than the lap models he currently made. He had converted a few regular acoustic guitars to electric for individual customers, but wanted to go further.

There's no hard evidence of who first thought of a Fender Spanish-style electric, although salesman Charlie Hayes may have suggested it to Leo. If he did, then it was by far the most important contribution he made to the company's prosperity, way beyond all the amplifiers and instruments that he sold and the dozens and dozens of dealers he signed up and encouraged.

Guitar-makers and musicians really didn't understand or appreciate the potential for electric guitars, which were still in their infancy. Rickenbacker, National, Gibson and Epiphone had made regular 'Spanish' archtop hollow-body acoustic guitars with f-holes and built-in electric pickups and associated controls since the 1930s, but to little effect. Rickenbacker was located in Los Angeles, not far from Fender, and had been the first with a pickup employing the then novel electro-magnetic principle – the type used since on virtually every electric guitar.

Gibson set the style for the best hollow-body electrics, launching for example the accomplished ES-175 in 1949. And while demand was rising from dance-band guitarists who found themselves increasingly unable to compete with the volume of the rest of the band, these early electric-acoustic guitars were mostly experimental, only partially successful from a technical standpoint, and still to become a great commercial sensation. A number of guitar makers, musicians and amateur inventors in America were wondering about the possibility of a solidbody instrument. Leo himself had already made one: that pickup testbed he'd built with Doc Kauffman in the early 1940s. But the attraction to players of a solidbody guitar was that it would cut the annoying feedback often produced by amplified hollow-body guitars. At the same time, a solid instrument would reduce the body's interference with the guitar's tone and so more accurately reproduce and sustain the sound of the strings. Leo explained later: "I wanted to get the sound you hear when you hold the head of an acoustic guitar against your ear and pluck a string."[16]

Rickenbacker had begun marketing a relatively solid Bakelite-body electric guitar in 1935 – the type that Doc Kauffman had played – but the guitar, offered in lap and Spanish forms, was small and awkward. Around 1940, in New York, guitarist Les Paul built his 'log', a personal testbed electric cobbled together from a number of instruments and centred on a solid through-neck block of pine. A little later he concocted a couple of similar instruments for regular playing, his 'clunkers'.

Taking a close look at Paul Bigsby's solidbody guitar

In Downey, California, about 15 miles to the west of Fender's operation in Fullerton, Paul Bigsby had a small workshop where he spent a lot of time fixing motorcycles and, later, making some fine pedal-steel guitars and vibrato units. He also ventured into solidbody electric guitars and mandolins. He hand-built a limited number of distinctive instruments, starting in 1948 with the historic Merle Travis guitar, a solidbody with through-neck construction (like Les Paul's and Leo's testbed guitars) and a headstock with the tuners all on one side (similar to the type seen on Martin and other German-influenced acoustic guitars of the early 19th century).

It seems unlikely that the design of the Fender solidbody was influenced very much by Bigsby's slightly earlier instruments. George Fullerton said that he and Leo knew Paul Bigsby and saw Merle Travis playing his Bigsby guitar, and Don Randall too said Leo had seen it. Travis himself has said that Leo borrowed his Bigsby, though Leo denied it. Dale Hyatt was probably right when he said he doubted there was any truth that Leo copied

Gearing up for a new kind of guitar

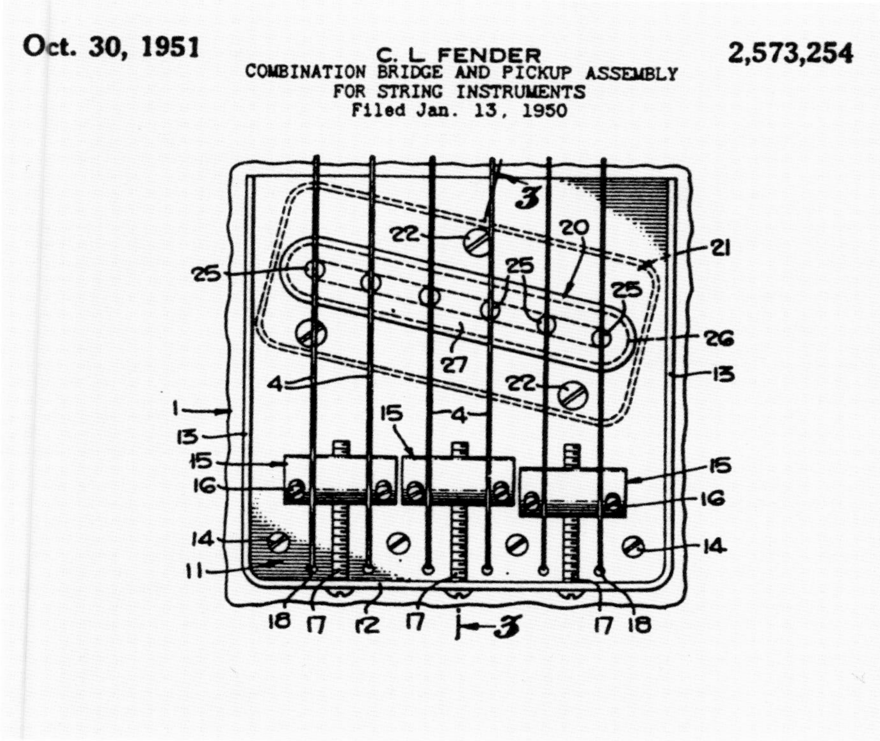

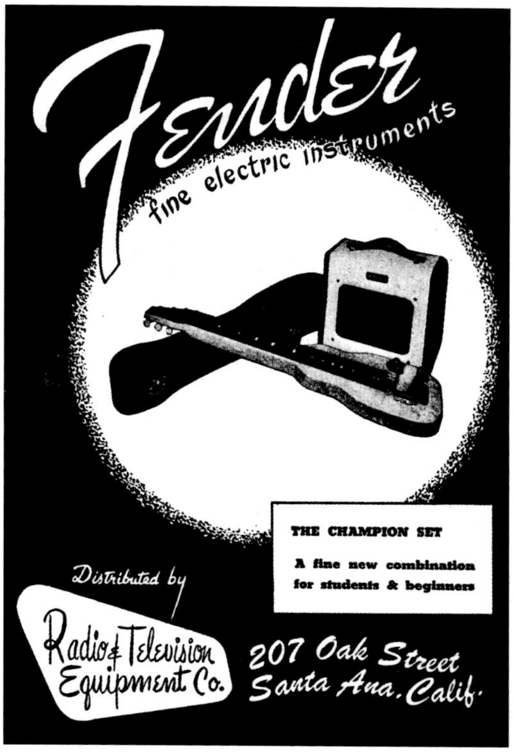

▲ **1948 Bigsby Merle Travis**

The Fender company was a modest operation at the end of the 1940s and into the early 1950s, producing a small number of lap steel guitars and amplifiers. The ad from 1949 pictured (above) features the Champion steel, which had a slanted pickup (patent drawing, above left) that would be used for the new solidbody guitar that became the Telecaster. Another early solidbody was the instrument that Paul Bigsby made for Merle Travis (main guitar), built in 1948 about 15 miles from Fender's HQ. Leo Fender soon gathered around him an impressive team of colleagues, including the company's sales head Don Randall, pictured opposite (centre) showing off a new bass in the early 1950s to a couple of trade-show visitors.

Paul Bigsby. "They just both made something at the same time."[17] Leo had his own ideas; the Bigsby simply proved that a guitar of this type could attract good musicians.

Some of the most important aspects of the design of the new solidbody Fender guitar would be adapted from the company's existing lap-steel instruments. The wonderful bridge pickup – arguably the key component of the classic Telecaster sound – was based on the unit already fitted to the Fender Champion steel, launched in 1949. The pickup was slanted to emphasise bass tones – just as Gibson had done with the pickup on their ES-300 model, introduced in 1940. The Fender bridge pickup would be recognised as one of the company's finest achievements, with a tone all of its own that would attract generations of players to the Telecaster and the Esquire.

"WE WANTED A STANDARD GUITAR THAT HAD A LITTLE BIT MORE OF THE SOUND OF THE STEEL GUITAR."
Leo discusses the tone of his new 'Spanish' electric

Leo decided to base the solid construction of the new guitar on the way he made his solid-wood steels. He wanted to maintain the advantages of these relatively easy-to-make guitars. There was absolutely no point, as far as he was concerned, to even consider the relatively complex methods used by contemporary electric guitar makers like Gibson and Epiphone. Their workers used many parts and a great deal of time and effort to construct hollow-body instruments. It's often been said that Fender's workshop was more like a furniture factory than an instrument factory. Expediency and straightforward practicality ruled Leo's head and, therefore, the Fender shop.

We've mentioned a few times now that Doc Kauffman had a Rickenbacker semi-solidbody guitar. The inquisitive Leo must have studied the design of his friend's instrument in detail and couldn't have failed to notice that the Rick had a detachable neck. He would have realised that this made sense for easy repair and service – he knew from the number of returns of some early Fender products how important this was – and a detachable neck would appeal to his love of simple, economic methods of working. National and Dobro also made their guitars with detachable necks, but along with Rickenbacker they were in the minority. Most mainstream makers employed the more time-consuming glued-on neck that needed the attention of skilled workers.

Leo knew that he could manufacture a solidbody electric guitar practically and cheaply. He knew that it would make sense to musicians and offer them musical advantages. "I guess you would say the objectives were durability, performance, and tone," he explained later. He looked again at his existing steels when he considered the kind of tone that the new 'standard' guitar ought to have. He said: "We wanted a standard guitar that had a little bit more of the sound of the steel guitar."[18]

Hollow-body electric guitars of the time generally delivered a warm, woody tone, reflecting the construction of the instrument and the position of a pickup near the neck.

Jazz guitarists loved that sound. Leo had something quite different in mind. Not for Fender the fat Gibson and Epiphone jazz voice. His lap-steels had a cleaner, sustained tone, and that's what he wanted for the new solidbody, something like a cross between a clear acoustic guitar and a cutting electric lap-steel.

As ever, he consulted many local musicians, trying out prototypes with them, putting testbed instruments in their hands, constantly asking their opinions on this pickup arrangement or that control set-up. One guinea pig said how he'd often turn around on stage at a local gig to see Leo "oblivious of musicians, audience, club management and disruption generally," busily changing amp controls or suggesting guitar settings – usually in mid-song.[19]

George Fullerton remembered spending many long hours at Leo's side as the design for the Telecaster came together. "How do you design something that's a brand new item, a brand new thing, that will fit people and be desirable? We tried a lot of different things and finally came up with the basic design," he said. "It seemed to be the most suitable thing we had found: easy to hold, easy to play, you could get to all the frets. Leo was very strong for building something that was very serviceable, durable, easy to repair, and, like he used to call it, 'built like a tank,' to stand up to rough treatment. We tried to design something that would be strong and do a good job for a playing musician. We made lots of different things that we tested and tried. We didn't just decide what to do and do it; it had to be proven."[20]

Working on the Fender prototypes

Two single-pickup prototypes for the new guitar have survived. The first one dates from the summer of 1949 and has a two-piece pine body. The headstock was based on the existing lap-steel guitars – symmetrical, slightly tapered, and with three tuners each side. The integral steel bridge/pickup assembly, the two-knob control plate, and the bolt-on neck were all in place. A second prototype from around the autumn or winter of 1949 was made from ash – which became a key timber for early Fender solidbody guitars – and had the remarkable six-tuners-on-one-side head that we know and love today as the Telecaster headstock. The new solidbody was nearly there.

> "LEO WANTED SOMETHING THAT WAS SERVICEABLE, DURABLE, EASY TO REPAIR, AND BUILT LIKE A TANK."
> *Fender's George Fullerton*

But Don Randall was frustrated. Leo did not have a finished sample good enough for Randall to take over to New York City to the NAMM show in summer 1949. At these important regular gatherings of the National Association of Music Merchants, major manufacturers would show off their new models, usually in advance of them appearing on the market. Dealers would visit from all over the country to decide which of the new wares they would eventually stock in their stores.

Starting life as an Esquire

In its earliest guise the new Fender solidbody electric was called the Esquire, as seen in the first advertisement to include the guitar (below) in 1950. The early pre-production sample is finished in black, like the Esquire that Spade Cooley's guitarist Jimmy Wyble plays in another 1950 ad (right). Western-swing fiddle star Cooley had a popular TV show with his band (pictured on set, left, with a Fender steel player). Guitarist Charlie 'Walkin The Guitar Strings' Aldrich was snapped by Leo in the new Fender factory in summer 1950 (opposite, bottom left) holding a blond one-pickup Esquire. Aldrich's early model was finished in the 'blond' natural colour that became the standard look for the Esquire, Broadcaster, and Telecaster.

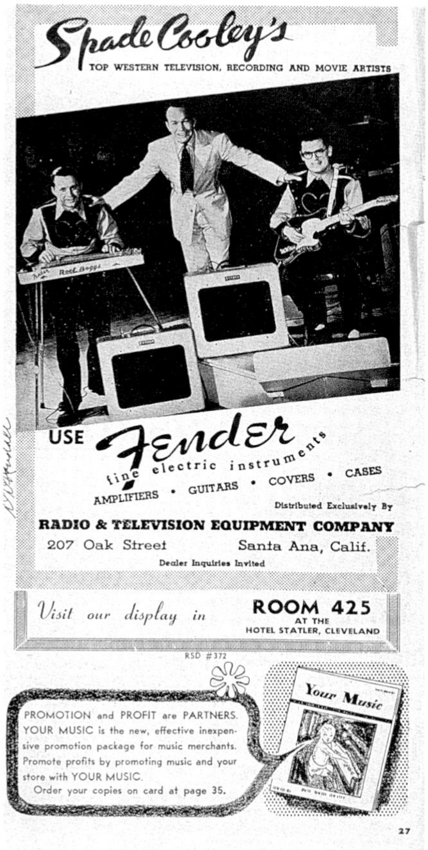

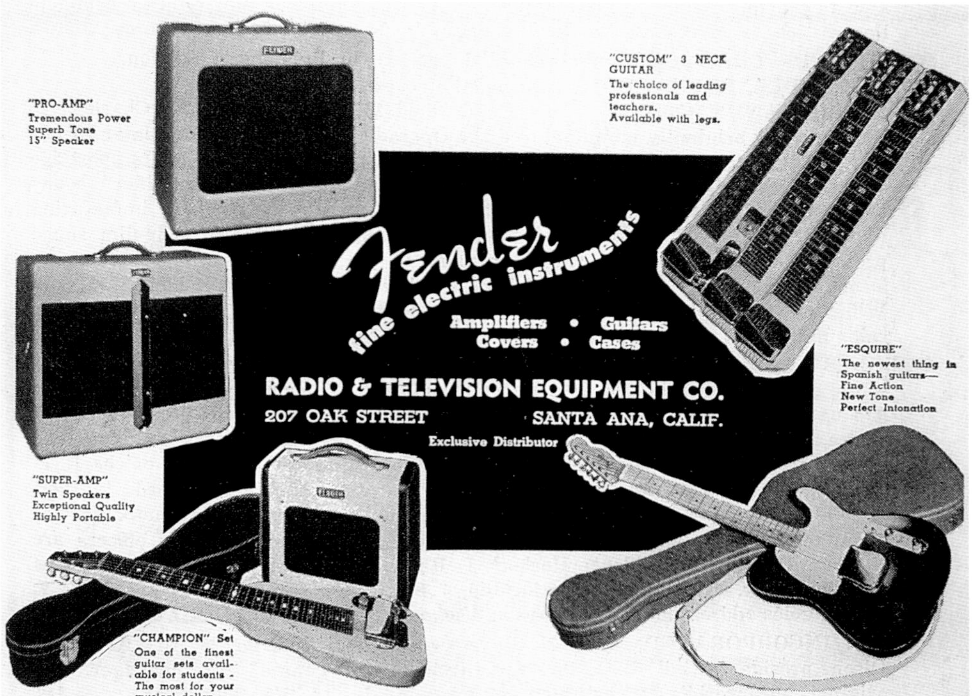

With time on his hands, the Fender sales boss took a good look around at the other makers' products. Randall lost no time in telling Leo his conclusion: a single pickup was simply not enough for the new guitar. He saw that Gibson was launching a new ES-5 hollow-body electric with no fewer than three pickups, and several other companies had two-pickup models at the New York show. Randall battled with Leo over the need for a two-pickup guitar. Fullerton again: "Leo was a really strong minded person with the ideas he had: you didn't change him. If he had an idea to try something, the only way you'd ever change him would be to prove that what he had would not work."[21] Reluctantly, Leo would end up with two new solidbody guitars: the single-pickup and (briefly) two-pickup Esquires and, slightly later, the two-pickup Broadcaster.

But first, by April of 1950, Fender had the new single-pickup instrument to promote in their catalogue. "The 'Esquire' guitar is something entirely new in the electric Spanish guitar field," wrote Randall, who named the new Esquire himself. "The features found in this new guitar are far in advance of all the competition." Today we're used to advertising hype; back then it was more or less the truth. Randall went on to highlight the attractions of the new-fangled construction. "Because the body is solid, there is no acoustic cavity to resonate and cause feedback as in all other box type Spanish guitars. The guitar can be played at extreme volume without the danger of feedback."[22]

Richard Smith charted much of this early history in his excellent book *Fender: The Sound Heard 'Round The World* and noted that Fender salesman Dave Driver got his sample of the new single-pickup Esquire on April 4th 1950, with his colleague Charlie Hayes receiving two on the 7th and the 15th. But production of solidbody guitars in any great numbers was yet to start at the Fender factory. The first appearance of the Esquire on a Fender pricelist came on August 1st, by now with two pickups, where it sat alongside six steel guitars and five amplifiers, pegged at $139.95. A case added a further $39.95. In May, Fender had added a new concrete building alongside the two steel ones on Pomona Avenue, presumably with increased production in mind.

"THE GENTLEMAN CAME DOWN TO MY BROTHER'S HOUSE AND BROUGHT HIS SON'S ELECTRIC TRAIN SET, WHICH HE WANTED TO TRADE FOR ONE OF THE GUITARS."
Salesman Dale Hyatt meets an early potential customer

The simple, effective Fender Esquire with its basic, single-cutaway solid slab of ash for a body and separate screwed-on maple neck was geared to mass production. The slanted pickup was mounted into a steel bridge-plate carrying three adjustable bridge saddles – for two strings each. The body was finished in a yellowish semi-transparent colour known as 'blond' (black on some early samples) and the pickguard was black. The guitar was plain. It was like nothing else and was ahead of its time. It fulfilled Leo's aim to have a standard guitar that was easy to build, and as such underlined one of the reasons for Fender's coming success. It was a relatively simple, unadorned guitar that served a practical purpose: it did exactly what the player wanted as soon as he plugged it into an amp.

But it did not prove immediately easy to sell, as Don Randall of Radio-Tel soon found out. This time when he went to the NAMM show – in Chicago in July 1950 – he had a sample of the new guitar with him. Randall represented Fender alongside salesmen Charlie Hayes and Don Patton at Radio-Tel's display in Room 795 at the Palmer House. "I just got laughed out of the place," said Randall. "Our new guitar was called everything from a canoe paddle to the snow shovel. There was a lot of derision."

Randall did have at least one useful meeting at the Chicago trade show, however, when Al Frost from National explained that the lack of neck strengthening in these samples would be likely to cause problems later for neck stability. "So I contacted Leo," Randall recalled, "and I says Leo, we've got to have a neck [truss] rod in there. [Leo said,] 'No we don't need one, it's rock maple.' I said I tell you one thing: either we put a neck rod in there or we don't sell it. Now make up your mind!

"And this was the way I had to handle Leo. He was actually kind of afraid of me; I don't know why. I was the only guy who could handle him and make him do things. Rest of them it was, Oh yeah Leo, yes Mr Fender. But Leo was about two-thirds afraid of me, because I really leaned on him to get him to make changes that were necessary. So we put out just a few of them without a neck rod, and then we put a neck rod in."[23]

Salesman Dale Hyatt also had to struggle against a less than serious view of these new Fenders he was trying to sell further north. He had his Esquire samples and was out hawking his wares in Manteca, just a few miles inland from San Francisco. Hyatt's brother, who lived in the area, had tipped him off about the dozens of country musicians playing around town – and it was country players who were showing most interest in the new Fender electric guitar.

"They had these nightclubs going and guys playing honky-tonk and country-western," Hyatt said of the scene in Manteca. "I'd taken five guitars with me. So I got a guy playing one. He quite liked it – and all of a sudden it just quit, didn't know what was wrong with it. It was embarrassing. So I went out to the truck, got another one. It lasted about 30 minutes and it quit. Then they started saying: 'There he goes again, ladies and gentlemen, wonder how many he's got?' Anyway, the third one kept on going and worked for the rest of the evening."

Hyatt had stumbled on a weakness of the new Fender's pickup shielding in the most public way imaginable. This was the cost of trying to sell what were still in effect pre-production versions, or working prototypes. "But anyhow, that was the start of it," Hyatt laughed. "That gentleman came down to my brother's house the next day and brought his son's electric train set, which he wanted to trade for one of the guitars.

"Another of the first ones sold of what we now know as the Telecaster – it might have been the second or third I sold, I'm not sure – was to a gentleman in Long Beach. He was one of the very first people to buy Leo Fender's solidbody guitar, and I know he played that thing for years and years."[24]

Broadcasting on all six strings

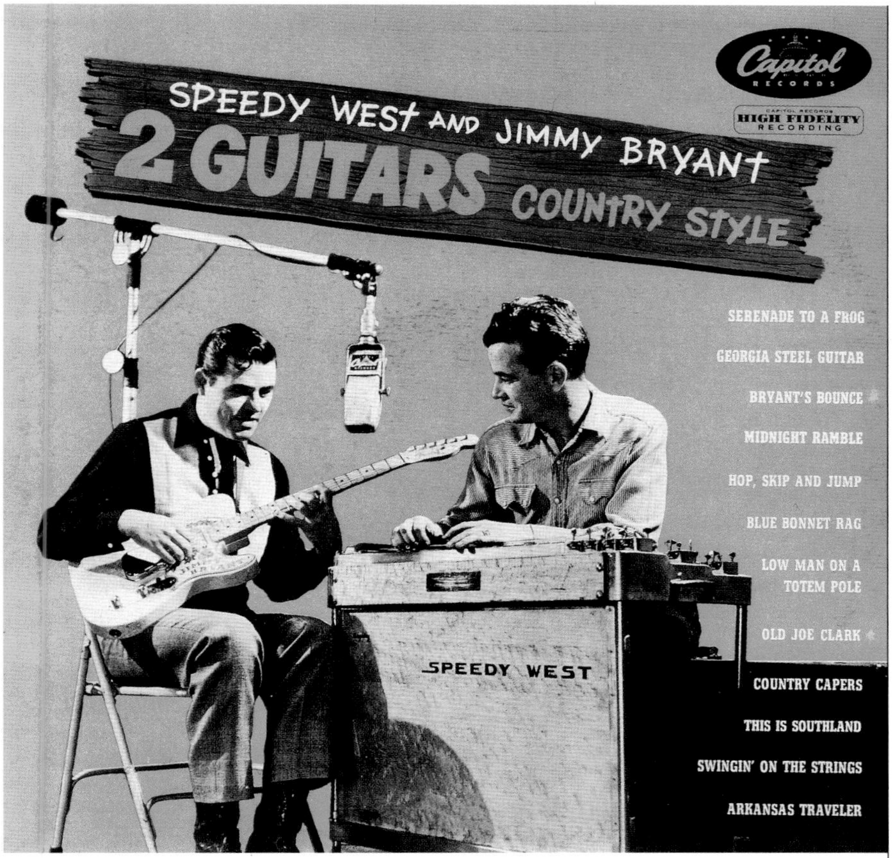

The Fender Broadcaster (main guitar) was the shortlived production model of Fender's new solidbody. Leo's old colleague Doc Kauffman is seen (opposite) at the Fender factory with a new Broadcaster in winter 1950/51. The Gretsch drum company objected to the use of 'Broadcaster' (they had Broadkaster drums) so Fender looked for a new name. In the meantime they snipped the headstock decal (below), resulting in 'Nocaster' guitars. One of the earliest notable players of Fender's new electric was Jimmy Bryant (above), often teamed with pedal-steel man Speedy West.

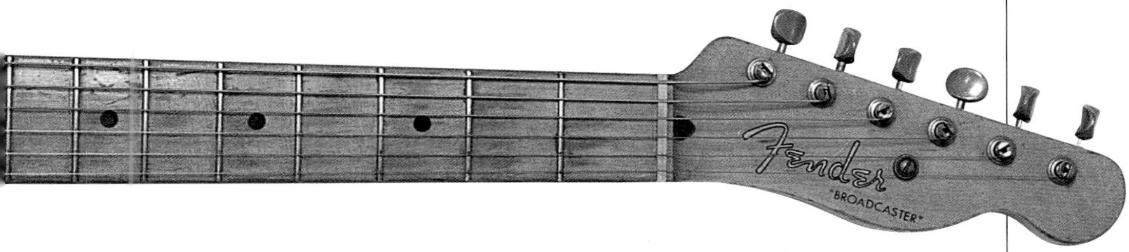

▲ **1950 Fender Broadcaster**

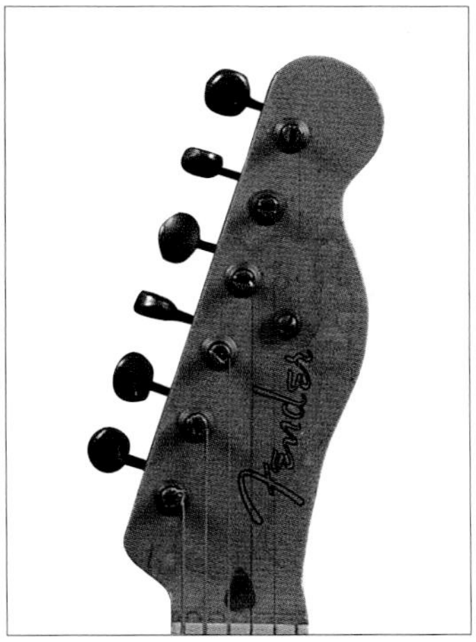

For now, the Esquire was put aside until proper production of the single-pickup model began in January 1951. But in October or November 1950 production started of a two-pickup Fender, now with added truss-rod following the trade-show advice and some more badgering of Leo by Randall. Randall came up with a new name, Broadcaster, and the retail price was set at $169.95. This put it around the same level as Gibson's fine ES-175 hollow-body electric, which sold for $175. In today's money, that would be equivalent to about $1,350, underlining the fact that these were not cheap guitars. The most basic new hollow-body electric from budget brands such as Silvertone, for example, could be had for around $40 ($300 in today's money).

The Broadcaster was really the first Fender solidbody electric to be made and sold in any reasonable numbers. Leo said later: "The single- and double-pickup guitars overlapped ... but the Broadcaster was the first one we built."[25] In other words, we can presume he meant this was the first one to be built in significant numbers. Richard Smith calculated that Fender sold 152 Broadcasters in the first two months of 1951. All this makes the Fender Broadcaster the historically significant solidbody electric guitar.

But the Broadcaster name was shortlived, halted in February 1951 after Gretsch, the large New York-based instrument manufacturer, indicated their existing use of 'Broadkaster' on drum products (and earlier on banjos). Gretsch had already stopped another drum company, Slingerland, from using the name, and evidently were sufficiently troubled by Fender's guitar to block that use too.

Fender complied with the request, as Dale Hyatt explained. "There was a sense of camaraderie between the manufacturers in the early days. No one was trying to beat the other to a patent or anything like that. So Gretsch just pointed it out and we agreed to do it."[26] This is echoed in Randall's letter dated February 21st 1951 to Fender salesmen, outlining the necessity of a name change. He told them that Gretsch had advised Fender of the infringement. "We have checked this and are inclined to agree that they are fair in their request," wrote Randall. "Consequently, it behooves us to find a new name. ... If any of you have a good name in mind I would welcome hearing from you immediately." At first, Fender simply used up their existing Fender Broadcaster decals on the guitar's headstock by cutting off 'Broadcaster' and leaving just the Fender logo. These no-name guitars are known today among collectors as Nocasters.

I name this guitar ... Telecaster

The new name for the Fender solidbody that Don Randall coined a few days later was Telecaster. (Randall subsequently came up with virtually all the well-known Fender guitar model names.) The Telecaster name certainly seemed appropriate, fresh from the new age of television and telecasts. Leo himself was well aware of the drawing power of TV, as George Fullerton explained. "When television was brand new, Leo's store was probably the only place in town that had televisions, and he used to have one that he'd put in the window facing out into the street, speaker outside. At night there'd be a crowd of people around watching wrestling or whatever was on. Sometimes it would be cold and foggy, but there'd still be this crowd of people."[27] The Telecaster name was on headstocks of the two-pickup model by April 1951, and at last Fender's new $189.50 solidbody electric had a permanent name. The single-pickup Esquire was also available by now and priced at $149.50. The solid case for either would add $39.95.

One of the earliest players to appreciate the new Fender sound was Jimmy Bryant, best known for his remarkable guitar instrumental duets with pedal-steel virtuoso (and Fender player) Speedy West. Bryant was also a busy Los Angeles session player and was a regular on Cliffie Stone's country TV showcase, *Hometown Jamboree*. If you've never heard Bryant before, prepare for a shock. You could do worse than start by listening to 'Bryant's Bounce' by Speedy West & Jimmy Bryant (1952), Tennessee Ernie Ford's 'Catfish Boogie' (1953), or even 'Oakie Boogie' by Ella Mae Morse (1952), each a glimpse at Bryant's clean, clever and sometimes wild, over-the-top playing that ever since has had fellow guitarists hardly believing their ears and wondering to themselves quite how he did it.

"GIVING A FENDER TO JIMMY BRYANT WAS LIKE STARTING A PRAIRIE FIRE. SOON WE COULDN'T MAKE ENOUGH OF THEM." *George Fullerton*

Leo and George Fullerton had taken an early Broadcaster out to the Riverside Rancho, a western-music nightclub in Glendale, California, where Bryant was playing. He took a look at this strange new guitar, picked it up, and started playing. Fullerton: "He got to do a lot of neat things on this guitar, and pretty soon all these people who'd been dancing were crowding around listening to what he was doing. It wasn't long before the whole band was standing around too. He was the centre of attention. Jimmy played things on guitar that nobody could play. And of course this was an electric with low action – and with that cutaway he could go right up the neck.

"So naturally we put one in his hand, and this was like starting a prairie fire. Pretty soon we couldn't make enough of those guitars. That wasn't the only reason, but it was a lot of it, because Jimmy was on television shows, personal appearances, and everybody wanted a guitar like Jimmy Bryant's. That was one of the starting points of that guitar."

Fullerton said that Fender guitars were aimed at the working musician. "Think of a movie cowboy and you might remember Roy Rogers, Gene Autry: the big silver screen, and here they are in their fancy hats and shirts and boots and their shiny gold-plated guns. But did you ever see a real working cowboy? He's dirty and got rough boots on and heavy leather on his pants. So we looked at the guitar players as being working cowboys. If you're gonna go out on stage for a personal appearance and you're a top-notch entertainer, you might want a flashy guitar and flashy clothing. But you're not a working musician, and that's not your dress code. See, this Telecaster was so popular – still is right today – and it's part of the musician's dress code. Take that away and put something else there and you're taking off part of their dress, part of their appearance. It's like taking Roy Rogers and not putting the hat on him. Putting a cap on him," he laughed.[28]

From henceforth thou art Telecaster

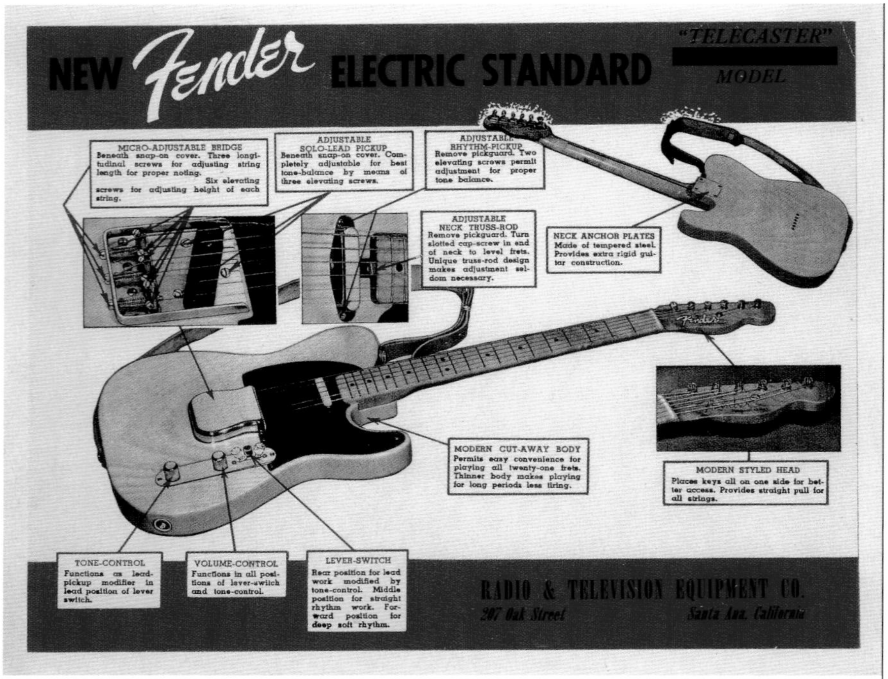

After Gretsch's request, Fender changed the name of the Broadcaster to Telecaster – and so was born the company's longest-running electric guitar model. Fender adapted existing promotional material (left) to reflect the new model name. The instrument pictured (main guitar) is typical of the earliest style of Telecaster. A 1951 patent for the Telecaster design (opposite, below) was drawn up by Fender's attorneys, while an early player who took to the Telecaster was Bill Carson. He is seen (opposite) among the line-up of Hank Thompson's band at the time of their 1952 hit 'The Wild Side Of Life'. Meanwhile, a Fender ad from that year (bottom right) underlines the availability of the new solidbody in two forms: single-pickup Esquire and two-pickup Telecaster.

HANK THOMPSON and his BRAZOS VALLEY BOYS
Nation's No. 1 Western Recording Artist Recording exclusively on Capitol Records
HANK THOMPSON
PAUL McGHEE
Nation's No. 1 Western Swing Band.
PERSONAL MANAGEMENT—
15½ S. WALKER, OKLAHOMA CITY, OKLA.
JIM HALSEY
PHONES—REGENT 6-8081, REGENT 6-0002

▾ 1953 Fender Telecaster

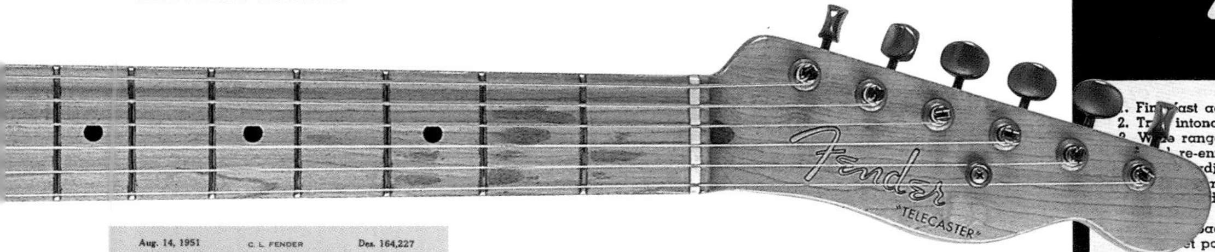
Fender
"TELECASTER"

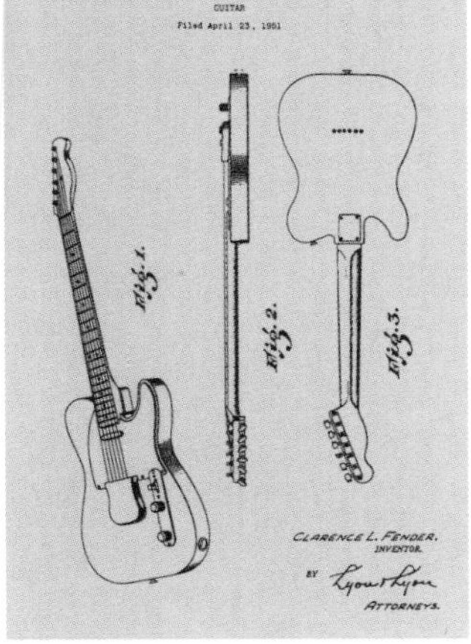

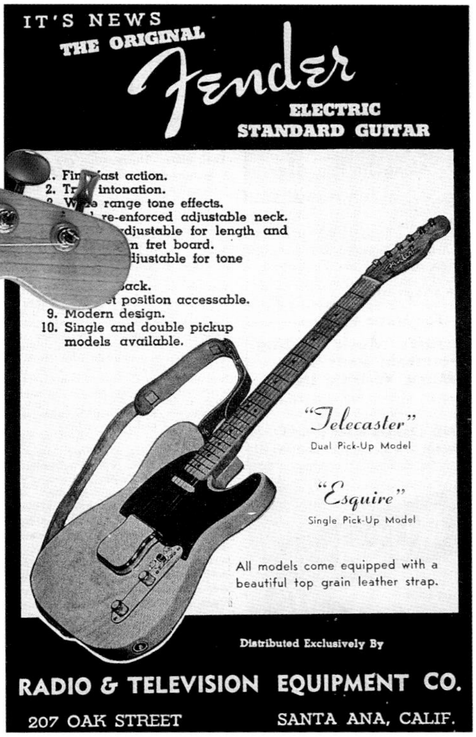
IT'S NEWS
THE ORIGINAL
Fender
ELECTRIC
STANDARD GUITAR
ast action.
intonation.
range tone effects.
re-enforced adjustable neck.
djustable for length and
n fret board.
djustable for tone
ack.
t position accessable.
9. Modern design.
10. Single and double pickup models available.
"Telecaster"
Dual Pick-Up Model
"Esquire"
Single Pick-Up Model
All models come equipped with a beautiful top grain leather strap.
Distributed Exclusively By
RADIO & TELEVISION EQUIPMENT CO.
207 OAK STREET
SANTA ANA, CALIF.

Fender launched a very important instrument in 1951, the Precision Bass – the first commercially successful solidbody electric bass guitar. (This was the exception to Randall naming the instruments; 'Precision' was Leo's idea.) Business began to pick up as news of the Telecaster spread and as Randall's five Radio-Tel salesmen – Charlie Hayes, Don Patton, Dave Driver, Mike Cole and Art Bates – began to persuade store owners to stock the company's new solidbody instruments.

Early in 1953 Fender's existing sales set-up with Radio-Tel was re-organised into a new Fender Sales distribution company, operational by June. Based like Radio-Tel in Santa Ana, Fender Sales had four business partners: Leo, Don Randall, Francis Hall and Charlie Hayes (the latter three coming from Radio-Tel). This was in fact the start of a power shift away from Hall.

Hayes, who had been Radio-Tel's first salesman, was killed in a road accident in 1955 (Dale Hyatt took over his sales patch, Fender's radio store having closed in 1951). Late in '53, Hall had effectively sealed his own fate by buying the Rickenbacker company – a potential competitor. So in 1955 Fender Sales changed to a partnership between Leo and Randall, though it was Randall who actually ran this pivotal part of the Fender business. As Dale Hyatt said, "You can make the finest guitar in the world, but if you don't sell the first one you're not going to get the chance to make another."[29]

Keeping faith with the amps and steels

Despite the exciting new developments with the solidbody guitar and bass, during the early 1950s Fender's main business remained in amplifiers and electric steel guitars. They were vitally important to the reorganised Fender operation, and the lines were rapidly expanded. Before 1950, the Fender amplifier line included early wooden-handled 'Model 26' versions of the Deluxe, Professional and Princeton models, as well as an angled-front twin-speaker model, the Dual Professional (soon renamed Super), and a remodelled series with 'TV-front' cabinets and Fender's famed tweed-pattern cloth covering.

In 1951 along came the Bassman amp, intended to amplify the new Precision but later highly regarded by guitar players. The following year saw another new item, the Twin Amp, this one aimed from the outset at guitarists. It became the top model in Fender's amplifier line, boasting 15 watts through twin 12-inch speakers in a new-design 'wide panel' cabinet. The whole amplifier line – including Bandmaster, Bassman, Deluxe, Princeton, Pro Amp and Super – was restyled to reflect the new look.

Fender's single-neck steels before 1950 included the Organ Button – an odd name derived from a switchable muted 'organ'-tone effect – plus the cheap Princeton with hardwired lead (cord), the long-lived Deluxe, which survived in various guises until 1980, and the Champion. The latter was renamed Student in 1952 as a come-on to the booming guitar-teaching 'studios' of the time that Randall recognised as a ready-made market. Fender had made multi-neck steel guitars from the earliest days: the two-neck Dual 8 Professional, for example, was launched in 1946, and the triple-neck Custom followed three years later. They provided players with the means to change relatively quickly between tunings, although the pedal-steel guitar would soon dispose of this rather unwieldy arrangement.

Western swing, a lively dance music that grew up in Texas dancehalls during the 1930s and '40s, had popularised the electric guitar in America, at first mostly with steel guitars. Many of the genre's steel players drew their driving electric guitar runs from Fender models such as the Stringmaster, notably Noel Boggs with Spade Cooley and Leon McAuliffe with Bob Wills. There were also some 'Spanish' guitarists like Telecaster-wielding Bill Carson with Hank Thompson's Brazos Valley Boys, who played a commercial fusion of western swing and honky tonk and had a 1952 Number 1 country hit with 'The Wild Side Of Life'. Spade Cooley's guitarist Jimmy Wyble was pictured with an Esquire in an early Fender ad.

As we've seen, the new single-pickup Esquire and two-pickup Telecaster were on sale from the early months of 1951, and these blond-finish models would be the target of a few changes over the rest of the decade. During 1952 a fundamental change was made to the wiring of the two-pickup control operation. The Tele had two metal knobs and a three-way selector switch. The front knob always controlled overall volume. Beyond that it got a bit tricky. Until the change, the two-pickup models were wired so that the selector in the rear position delivered both pickups, with the rear knob controlling the amount of neck-pickup sound blended into the bridge-pickup sound. The selector in the other two positions delivered neck-pickup only with preset tone: in the middle position with a 'natural' tone and in the front position a bassier tone; the rear knob made no difference to either.

During 1952 the set-up was changed. In the new two-pickup system, shoving the selector into the rear position delivered the bridge pickup alone, with the rear knob acting as a proper tone control, while the middle position gave neck pickup alone, also with proper tone control. In the front position the effect was the same as the old system, in other words neck-pickup alone with a preset bassier tone and a non-functioning rear knob. This meant that for now (and until the late 1960s) there was no both-pickups setting. As we'll see, some players soon discovered 'secret' settings between the selector switch's official stops.

"YOU CAN MAKE THE FINEST GUITAR IN THE WORLD, BUT IF YOU DON'T SELL THE FIRST ONE, THEN YOU'RE NOT GOING TO GET THE CHANCE TO MAKE ANOTHER."
Dale Hyatt, Fender salesman

The single-pickup Esquire also had an odd control system. Again, there were two metal knobs and a three-way selector switch, with the front knob always controlling overall volume. The selector in the rear position gave the pickup direct, with the rear knob changing nothing. The middle position gave what you'd expect of a simple single-pickup guitar: the pickup through volume and tone controls. The front position provided a preset bassier tone, again with a non-functioning rear knob.

On both the Telecaster and the Esquire the original black pickguard was changed to white in 1954. The following year the guitars gained staggered polepieces on the bridge

From B.B. to Guitar Boogie

▲ 1952 Fender Esquire

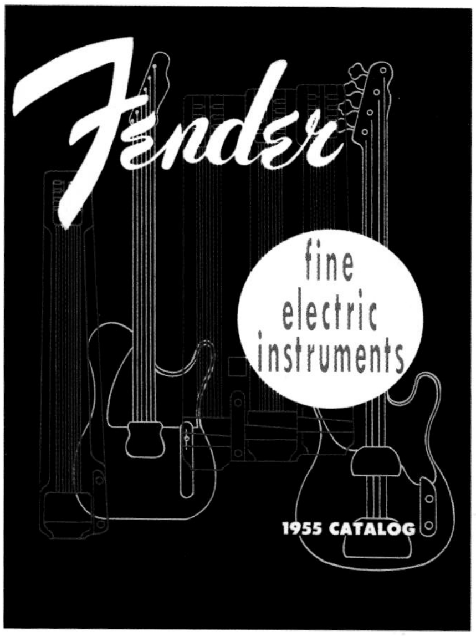

Leo Fender liked nothing better than to buy and try out new machines for his factory, such as the punch press that he stands alongside in the 1950s photograph opposite. As the decade progressed, Leo's company continued to make steel guitars, amplifiers ... and the new solidbody electric models, the one-pickup Esquire and the two-pickup Telecaster. A young B.B. King is pictured here clutching an early Esquire, and the main guitar on these pages is a fine early Esquire, still with the black pickguard that would change to white a few years later on both Esquire and Telecaster. A flyer published inside *Down Beat* magazine in July 1955 (opposite, centre) included Arthur 'Guitar Boogie' Smith on the cover with a Telecaster. The front of Fender's official 1955 catalogue (above) revealed a more impressive design, although the stylised outline of a Telecaster remained as one of the cover stars.

pickup, giving a slighter tougher sound, and the serial number was stamped on the neck-plate rather than the bridge-plate. An easy way to empty your bank account in the 21st century is to opt for one of the wonderful all-original black-'guard maple-neck Teles dating from the crucial early years of production.

Back in the 1950s, other makers at first merely continued to mock Fender's unique solidbody guitars. But soon Gibson had joined in with its Les Paul, Gretsch with the Duo Jet, Kay with a K-125 model. At Fender, the sales side of the business was now under the control of Don Randall and his team, but another important addition came in 1953 when steel guitarist Freddie Tavares joined the California guitar maker, mainly to help Leo design new products.

IF THE GUITAR CRAZE HADN'T TAKEN OFF, LEO WOULDN'T HAVE MADE IT. GENIUS HAS TO HAVE SOME LUCK – AND HE HAD BOTH." *Karl Olmsted*

Tavares was best known for his swooping steel intro over the titles of the *Looney Tunes* cartoons. He later explained the working methods in Fullerton. "When it was just Leo and me, we did what we pleased. In other words Leo did what he pleased, and I was just his assistant."[30] A colleague described Tavares, who died in 1990, as "one of the best musicians I have ever known, and just as good at engineering. A very talented man".[31]

In June 1953 Fender acquired a three-and-a-half-acre plot at South Raymond Avenue and Valencia Drive in Fullerton with three new buildings. Fullerton's City Council was on a programme of rapid and significant industrial development. "Prior to 1950," reported the *Los Angeles Times*, "Fullerton was a citrus area with its industries primarily devoted to citrus products and food processing."

The paper quoted a Fullerton official on the changes being made in the new decade. "Everyone liked the peaceful area geared to country living. But some began to realise that industry was needed to balance the economy as more and more people came in. Now there's almost 100 percent support for it."[32]

Clearly, the new Fender buildings in the heart of Fullerton's development area indicated that expansion of the firm's products was imminent. As well as the two electric guitars, the Telecaster and Esquire, Fender had a line of seven amplifiers (Bandmaster, Bassman, Champ, Deluxe, Princeton, Super, Twin Amp), five electric steel guitars (Custom, Deluxe, Dual, Stringmaster, Student) and the Precision Bass.

But the company wanted to produce even more. *The Music Trades* magazine reported that with the new property Fender "hoped that production will be upped by almost 100 percent in the next few months".[33] First, however, their rather haphazard production methods had to be organised more efficiently.

This job fell into the very capable hands of another newcomer, Forrest White, who had worked as an industrial engineer at an aircraft firm in Akron, Ohio. During a business trip to Los Angeles in 1944 he'd fallen in love with the area and determined to move there.

White had built several guitars in his spare time, including an early solidbody electric ("way before Leo did," he claimed later).

White's opportunity to move out west came in 1951 when he was hired by a Los Angeles company. He'd already met Leo a few times, and in spring 1954 they had lunch. Leo asked White if he'd be interested in helping him sort out some "management problems" at Fender. White remembered their conversation. "Freddie Tavares had told Leo that the company was ready to go down the drain, it was that bad. Leo had no credit whatsoever, and had to pay cash buying any material and so on. Some of the employees' cheques were bouncing. Freddie had said that Leo didn't have anyone in the plant who could do what needed to be done. So it just so happened that my timing was right."[34]

Karl Olmsted of Race & Olmsted, Fender's tool-and-die maker, recalled how close Fender came to going broke at the time. "He tried to buy us with stock, to get out of paying our bills, and like idiots we didn't take the bait," Olmsted said with hindsight. "But actually I'm not sorry that I didn't, because I'm not sure that I could have worked for Leo day in, day out. At least we had the advantage of occasionally being able to say, 'Leo, this is all we can take,' and stepping back. As good as the relationship was, once in a while you had to do that – and I couldn't if they'd taken us over. We just gave him credit and credit and credit – practically to the point where we couldn't make our payroll and bills and everything else. If this guitar craze hadn't taken off, he wouldn't have made it. So genius has to have some luck – and he had both."[35]

Meanwhile, Leo took an intrigued Forrest White to look at Fender's set-up at the new South Raymond buildings. "And it was a mess," White recalled. "There was no planning whatsoever, because Leo was not an engineer, he was an accountant. Things had just been set down any place. Man, everything was just so mixed up, you can't believe it. There was no planning whatsoever, because in all fairness to him he didn't have any experience in things like that."

So White agreed to come in and work for Leo, beginning in May 1954. "But I said it depends on one thing. If I can have a free hand to do what I know has to be done, fine. Otherwise I'm not interested. He gave me that free hand. When I stepped in, from that point on I ran the company. He stayed in design, but I ran it."

One of the most important aspects of production that White clarified was an incentive scheme tied to quality control, where assemblers on the production line did not accept a product from the previous stage unless they were happy that it was perfect – effectively making each operator an inspector. "The reason for that," White explained, "was that if something had to be re-worked, it was on their own time. If someone loused up, hey – once they accepted it, then it's their problem. But as long as they turned out good production that passed, they made good money, darned good money."[36]

Now Leo had able men – Forrest White and Don Randall – poised at the head of the production and sales halves of the Fender company. He had a new factory, and a small but growing reputation. And he had the start of a fresh generation of guitars – the solidbody Telecaster, Esquire, and Precision Bass – with Freddie Tavares ready to help him

The Tele train keeps a-rollin'...

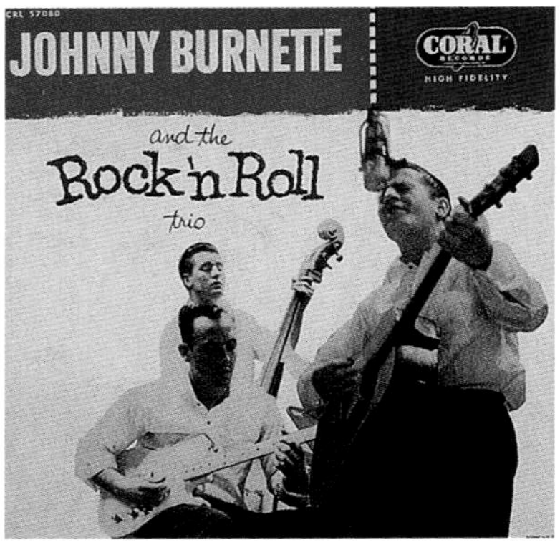

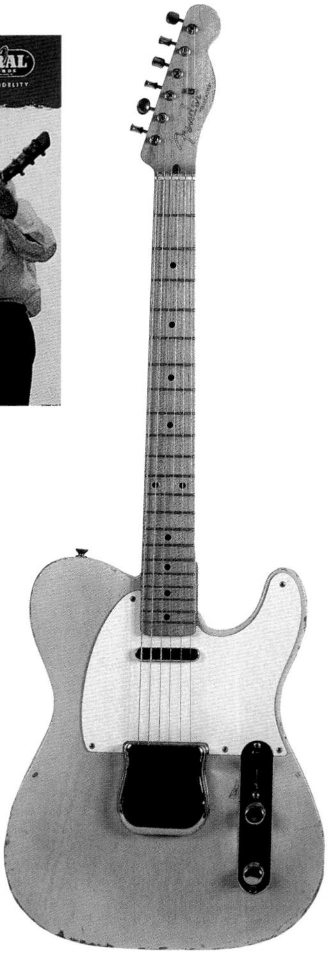

▶ 1956 Fender Telecaster

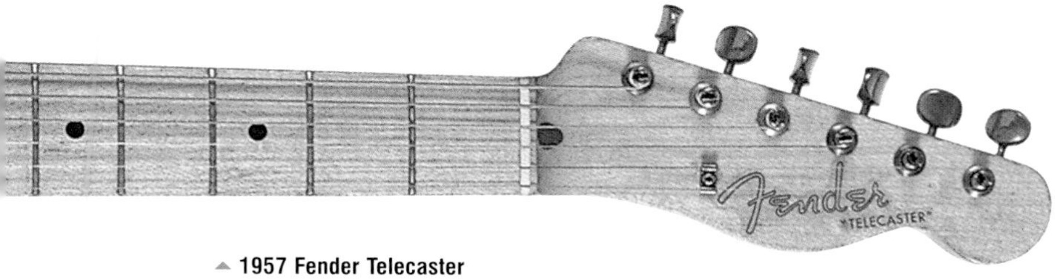

▲ **1957 Fender Telecaster**

By the mid 1950s the Tele and Esquire had moved to a white pickguard from the old black style, shown to good effect by the fine pair of Teles pictured on thse pages. As well as the new pickguard, they show the modified colour finish that Fender was using by that time. Teles were beginning to attract R&B and rock'n'roll action. Clarence 'Gatemouth' Brown (opposite, top left) played an attractive Texan mix of R&B and western swing on his Fender, while Paul Burlison in The Rock 'N Roll Trio (album sleeve, opposite) found a new, more angry voice with the aid of a distorted amp on their classic 'The Train Kept A-Rollin'', later covered by The Yardbirds. Guitarist Russell Willaford briefly played his Tele with Gene Vincent's Blue Caps (above) in the 1956 movie *The Girl Can't Help It*.

design new ones. Being Leo Fender, he was not content to stay still. Soon he and the team and the guinea pigs were working on a new guitar, one that would be released in 1954 as the Stratocaster.

In fact, Leo thought that the new, improved model would necessarily replace the Telecaster. Not quite. Fender's new Stratocaster did not have an immediate impact, and only later in rock'n'roll did it find its true home. Author Richard Smith has calculated that during 1954 and '55 Fender sold 720 Strats and 1,027 Teles. As we'll see, those proportions would fluctuate during the coming years.

Forrest White said that the manufacturing process for electric guitars was simple and effective at Fender in the 1950s. "We bought our lumber in long lengths, 18 or 20 feet, ash or alder, depending on what we were making. We'd make the Telecasters out of ash because of their almost transparent blond finish. You'd cut the wood and glue it together so you'd have a block of wood that was the size of a guitar body.

"Then we had what we called router plates made out of quarter-inch steel in the shape of the guitar body, usually two different plates. You'd attach one to the bottom with a couple of screws, and you could drill on that side, where the neck plate and everything went. On the other side went the plate where the pickups and everything ran. So you always had a minimum of two plates, sometimes three depending on how sophisticated the instrument was – some might have more cut-outs and so on. You'd screw those on, trace around them, band-saw the body roughly to shape, then take off the excess on the router, and on it would go for sanding.

"Then the necks. For ovalling [or shaping] you had a couple of holders swinging back and forth, and then there was a mandrel that had the holes cut out for the frets. Leo designed almost all of the tooling himself. It was very simple, but it was a case of having to walk before you ran. We didn't have any computerised routers and so on like they have now, where they can cut out half a dozen necks at a time. It was one at a time back then, and everything was simple. Crude, really, but it got the job done."[37]

There were more crude machines throughout Fender's factories. Some were for winding pickups – Heath Robinson affairs with wheels and pulleys – while another area housed a few ad hoc finish-spray booths alongside a wall of racks for drying sprayed bodies. There were punch presses for making metal parts. Then there were some benches for final assembly. For Telecasters, one worker would screw on pickguards and the neck pickup and fit the bridge/pickup unit and Kluson tuners, and then another would take over and solder the electronics together. Finally, new Teles would be strung up and tested through a handy amp lifted from the line.

For the time being, Fender continued to advertise and sell its established lines. Steel guitars continued virtually unchanged, but innovations were still being introduced for the ever-popular amplifiers. A new effect was tremolo, as Fender called it – a regular, rhythmic fluctuation in volume, previously heard on home organs. The amp that introduced this to the Fender line was the Tremolux, a 15-watt amp with single 12-inch speaker, launched in 1955. A pair of cheaper new solidbody guitars were added alongside the Telecaster,

Esquire and Stratocaster in 1956, the one-pickup Musicmaster and two-pickup Duo-Sonic, described in the company's literature as "three-quarter size" and thus "ideal for students and adults with small hands". An unusual solidbody electric Mandolin was also new in the company's catalogue.

By now there were over 50 people working at Fender and the factory was humming with constant activity. Work would sometimes spill out into the alleyways, a distinct advantage of the California climate. But Leo was almost always inside, and would often burn the midnight oil. The Telecaster was already proving itself a useful tool. Soon it would no longer be a matter of Fender trying to sell the guitars, but of making enough to meet the apparently ever-growing demand. With rock'n'roll around the corner, Fender's place in music history was but a few short years away.

James & Dale & Suzie & Ricky & Ozzie & Harriet

We've already met one notable Tele player, Jimmy Bryant – but for all his untamed dexterity he could hardly be described as rock'n'roll. Neither could B.B. King, who used a Telecaster around 1951 when he first went out on the road, nor Gatemouth Brown on early-'50s instrumentals such as 'Okie Dokie Stomp'. But the most visible player of the Tele later in the decade was James Burton, seen almost every week playing alongside rock'n'roller Ricky Nelson on the *Adventures Of Ozzie & Harriet* TV show. Back in 1953, a 13-year-old Burton had persuaded his parents to buy him a brand new Telecaster that he'd spied in a local store. He's been a top Tele man ever since and a prime influence on many other key players.

Burton may well have had the first Telecaster-fuelled Top 40 hit when his guitar lick turned into Dale Hawkins's raw 'Suzie Q', a song that crashed into the chart in July 1957, bursting with Burton's earthy playing. At the end of that year came the offer to join Ricky Nelson on the TV show. Burton, already a busy session player in Los Angeles, played rhythm guitar on his first Nelson sessions, but the first on which he played lead was 'Believe What You Say'. He said: "Back then you played it and mixed it at the same time. I got a great sound through my Fender Deluxe amplifier. It was a slinky, spacey, energetic sound. We were into rock'n'roll, and it was rocking. It jumped right out at you!"

'Believe What You Say' was a Number 4 hit for Ricky Nelson in April 1958 and marked the start of Burton's supreme string-bending skills, aided by an experimental set of strings. "I had the first, second, third and fourth as banjo strings. The third was unwound, which gave a much different sound to the regular wound string. I had the fifth and sixth as guitar strings, but with a D-string for where the A would be, and the E-string was an A – so I got them down to match with the light strings from the banjo. If you go back and listen to those early Ricky Nelson records you'll hear the difference."

From that point Burton played lead guitar on all Nelson's hits. Further experimentation came later when he discovered extra sounds among the Tele's controls. "You know the three-way switch that you had back then? I was just plucking the strings, and I noticed that when you moved the switch from the middle position to your lead pickup, in between

Muddy won't part with his either

Muddy Waters was one of the great Telecaster players, seen here (left) with his famous red instrument. He bought the guitar in the late 1950s, later adding a rosewood-board neck and that new finish. (He's pictured capo'd up and ready to go at a 1960s session with label owner Leonard Chess, Little Walter, and Bo Diddley.) While players such as Muddy were giving Fender high visibility on stage, the company upped their promo power when they hired a new ad agency in 1957, and specifically Bob Perine. His most famous innovation was the humorous series of 'You Won't Part With Yours Either' ads, starring Fender guitars in the most unlikely situations. Two typical examples are shown above, while the 1959 amplification ad (right) demonstrates that almost any Fender ad of the Perine period could boast a dose of charm and style.

the setting I got this particular sound. The volume was much lower, but the sound was very interesting. I always call it my little Chinese tone. Very plucky, very percussive."[38] Listen to his typically concise solo on the 1961 Number 1 'Travelin' Man' for a perfect example. We'll be hearing from Burton again later.

Some of Ricky Nelson's hits were written by Johnny and Dorsey Burnette, who'd been part of The Rock'n'Roll Trio. Paul Burlison blasted out on a loose-tube-distorted Telecaster on their sweaty and influential 1956 single 'The Train Kept A-Rollin'', later covered by The Yardbirds and others.

Meanwhile, some session players working in key American recording studios picked up Telecasters to get a sound they found increasingly in demand during the 1950s. Howard Roberts, Tommy Tedesco and Barney Kessel all bought Teles. Kessel, described as "the busiest session guitar man in Hollywood", was a jazzer much more at home with a hollow-body Gibson. In a 1956 interview he sounded distinctly uncomfortable about the new arrival. "I had to buy a special 'ultra toppy' guitar," he complained, "to get that horrible electric guitar sound that the cowboys and the rock'n'rollers want."[39]

Luther Perkins played a Telecaster on Johnny Cash's records, providing what Cash described as "one-string rhythm" and starting with the definitive 1956 hit 'I Walk The Line'. The record showed that the Tele could highlight bright, bassy lines at the heart of simple, direct pop music. In this it would prove to be something of a blueprint.

Muddy Waters and the walls of electrified sound

British players got their first remarkable glimpse of a real live Telecaster in October 1958 when Muddy Waters visited, bringing from Chicago his piano player Otis Spann ... and his Fender Telecaster. The sonic bombardment of real, loud, aggressive R&B came as a shock to many in the London audiences. "There were some who could not hear [Muddy's] voice properly over the powerfully amplified guitar, and others who simply do not care for the electric instrument at all," wrote a baffled reviewer. "I liked some of the violent, explosive guitar accompaniment – although there were times when my thoughts turned with affection to the tones of the acoustic guitar heard on his first record. ... Muddy seemed able to forget where he was standing as, eyes closed, he built up patterns, sometimes walls, of electrified sound."[40]

Muddy's "walls of electrified sound" were transforming the blues and bringing it ever closer to rock, a development that would reach fruition in the following decade. He stuck to his white-'guard maple-neck '57 Telecaster throughout the rest of his career, adding along the way a new red finish, a wider rosewood-board neck, and a high nut and bridge to aid his killer slide work. "What would I look like with two or three guitars like these kids?" he joked with an interviewer years later. "I don't need to be bothered with that. I got my one old guitar."[41]

Back at Fender, most of the work on the early publicity and ads had fallen to Don Randall, but during the 1950s it was clear that help was needed to take the brand to a new level. Advertising in America was becoming a more sophisticated affair, and smart agencies were adept at convincing firms to spend more on slick ads that provided a uniform identity for a set of products.

Fender turned to Bob Perine from the Perine-Jacoby agency of Newport Beach, California, in 1957. He would continue to shape the look of Fender publicity until 1969. Perine, a keen amateur guitarist himself, transformed Fender's image and in the process created some of the most stylish and memorable guitar ads and catalogues ever printed. Some collectors today seem to value prime 'Fender paper' of the 1950s and '60s almost as highly as the instruments themselves.

One of Perine's early tasks was to devise and shoot a series of press ads with a single idea: a Fender product in an unlikely setting, set off with the tag line "You won't part with yours either". In other words, your Fender guitar or amp is so important to you, you'll take it anywhere. One of the very first appeared in print toward the end of 1957 and showed a gent in a sharp suit on the top deck of a bus holding on tight to his white-finish white-'guard maple-neck Tele, as well he might. Many ads followed in the 'You won't part' series, along with others bearing the alternative line "Wherever you go you'll find Fender". Guitars were seen perched on army tanks, erect at the drive-in cinema, in mid-air around a skydiver's neck, strapped to a surfer … in fact, pretty much anywhere. Perine and his team must have had a lot of fun.

"WHAT WOULD I LOOK LIKE WITH TWO OR THREE GUITARS LIKE THESE KIDS? I GOT MY ONE OLD GUITAR."
Muddy Waters on his Telecaster

The Fender catalogues too suddenly became beautiful objects under the new man's direction. The 1958/59 catalogue was Fender's first with a full-colour front-and-back cover, which opened out to display a luscious panorama of prime gear, including a blond Tele and Esquire eyed up by one of two cool crewcutted chaps. The booklet was a model of clear, simple design. No matter that the pictures of the Tele and Esquire inside were of obsolete black-'guard models: you couldn't help but want everything, no matter what the details. But one new fact tucked alongside the Esquire might have particularly caught your eye: "Telecaster and Esquire guitars are available in custom color finishes at an additional 5% cost," it said.

All Fenders were now officially available in 'custom colors' beyond the regular finishes. This would explain the red Stratocaster proudly displayed on the front of that colourful 1958/59 catalogue. Most Fenders of the 1950s had come in a standard finish only: blond for Teles and Esquires, sunburst for Strats. Nonetheless a few guitars, specially made at the factory effectively as one-offs, were finished in solid colours. The rare surviving examples indicate that this practice was underway by 1954, but few players back then seemed to want a coloured guitar, and Fender's main production remained in blond and sunburst instruments. A handful of rare '50s Strats came in solid colours, but Telecasters hardly at all, though some special-order Teles of the period were finished in sunburst.

Red is the colour of my true love's axe

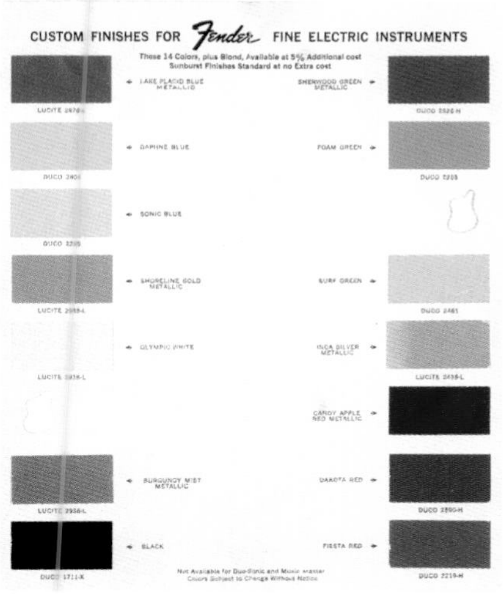

While the 1958/59 catalogue cover (left) still featured maple-neck guitars in mostly standard finishes, the big news from Fender was coloured paint and rosewood 'boards, seen in splendid confluence on our lovely Esquire (main guitar). A subtler change was the shift from five to eight pickguard screws in '59. Coloured guitars had been available from Fender for some time, but now there was an official line of Custom Colors, yours to choose from a specially devised finish chart (above). Rosewood upstaged maple during 1959, and Fender's ad from December that year (right) reflects the move to the new fingerboard wood – if not a new way to display the guitars.

Fender . . . the choice of student and professional musicians everywhere!
SOLD BY LEADING RETAIL MUSIC DEALERS THROUGHOUT THE WORLD
Left to right: Esquire, Telecaster Custom, Duo Sonic, Telecaster, Electric Mandolin,
Esquire Custom, Jazzmaster, Str ster, Musicmaster and Electric Precision Bass.
Left-hand instruments and
Fender SALES, INC.
SANTA ANA, CALIF

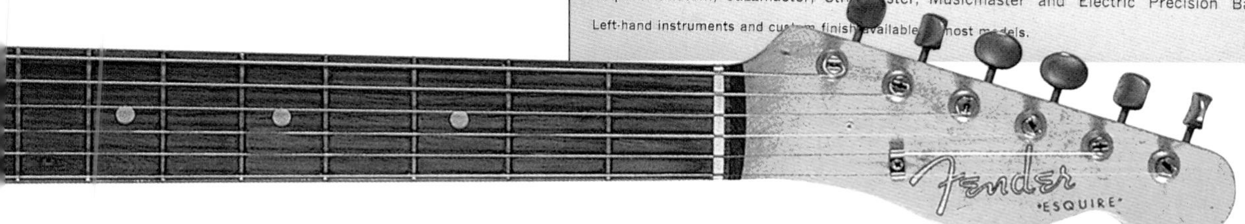

▲ **1959 Fender Esquire fiesta red**

The production of these early special-colour guitars was certainly casual. But the informal arrangement was first given a rather more commercial footing in the company's sales literature of 1956 when 'player's choice' coloured guitars were noted as an option, at five percent extra cost. In the following year these Du Pont paint finishes were described in Fender's catalogue as "Custom Colors" (a name that has stuck ever since) and in the pricelist as "custom Du Pont Duco finishes", still at five percent on top of regular prices.

Fender eventually came up with a defined list of the officially available Custom Colors, and in the early 1960s when many more Custom Color Fenders were being made the company even issued colour charts to publicise and help selection of the various shades. (Of the first three charts the original, in 1961, featured Black, Burgundy Mist Metallic, Dakota Red, Daphne Blue, Fiesta Red, Foam Green, Inca Silver Metallic, Lake Placid Blue Metallic, Olympic White, Shell Pink, Sherwood Green Metallic, Shoreline Gold Metallic, Sonic Blue, and Surf Green.

The second, in 1963, had lost Shell Pink and gained Candy Apple Red Metallic. The third, in 1965, lost Burgundy Mist Metallic, Daphne Blue, Inca Silver Metallic, Sherwood Green Metallic, Shoreline Gold Metallic, and Surf Green, and gained – all Metallics – Blue Ice, Charcoal Frost, Firemist Gold, Firemist Silver, Ocean Turquoise, and Teal Green.)

"TELECASTER AND ESQUIRE IN CUSTOM COLOR FINISHES AT ADDITIONAL 5% COST."
Late-1950s Fender catalogue

The automobile industry clearly had a profound effect on American guitar manufacturers in the 1950s, not least in this ability to enhance the look of an already stylish object with a rich, sparkling paint job. In fact the Gretsch company in New York had been the first guitar maker to adopt colourful car paints as standard colours for guitar models, creating new-look electric instruments such as the 'Cadillac Green' Country Club and the 'Jaguar Tan' Streamliner, both in 1954.

Du Pont was the biggest supplier of paint to the car factories, notably General Motors. Fender used paints from Du Pont's Duco nitro-cellulose lines, such as Fiesta Red or Foam Green, as well as the more colour-retentive Lucite acrylics like Lake Placid Blue Metallic or Burgundy Mist Metallic. As Custom Color researcher Clay Harrell has established, the names that Fender gave to the colours mostly came from the original car makers' terms: Fiesta Red, for example, was first used by Ford in 1956 for a Thunderbird colour, while Lake Placid Blue originally appeared on a 1958 Cadillac Brougham. Candy Apple Red, however, was a Fender original and not a car colour.

George Fullerton remembered going out to a local paint store around 1957, buying a Fiesta Red mix, and then going back to the factory and applying it to a guitar body. He insisted that this experiment was what started Fender's defined Custom Color line. "That first one became Fiesta Red," said Fullerton. "The Du Pont company made that colour and you could buy it right across the counter. That should have been a patent, that colour, but who knows at the time you do a thing? Meanwhile, the sales office and Don Randall laughed at it, said who in hell wants a coloured guitar, specially a red one."[42] Don Randall had a different recollection of the genesis of Fender's Custom Color line. "Gretsch had their Country Club which was green, the White Falcon which was white, and there were others. So it was just my idea to diversify and get another product on the market. They didn't sell as well as the traditional sunburst and blond colours."[43]

Whatever the origins of Fender's Custom Colors, decades later the guitars bearing these original Fiesta Reds, Sonic Blues, Burgundy Mists and the like have proved very desirable among collectors, and many of us rate a Custom Color Fender, especially an early one, as a prime catch. And we know that coloured Telecasters are particularly rare. All this despite the prevalence of 'refinishes' that recently have become so accurate that even alleged experts can be fooled into declaring some fake finishes as original. How much is a coat of paint worth?

Back at Fender in the 1950s, more changes were underway. Four new factory buildings and a warehouse were added to the South Raymond site in 1958, and by the following year the number of employees topped the 100 mark. As usual, a few small cosmetic and production adjustments were being made to the company's electric guitars, including the addition of three screws to the Tele and Esquire's pickguards in 1959, making a total of eight. This later provided a useful visual clue to tell quickly – fakes aside – between a 1950s and a '60s model.

A more peculiar modification was made to the Telecaster and Esquire during 1958 when the strings were anchored at holes in the back of the bridge-plate instead of passing through the body as usual. Quite what prompted this is unknown, but it was probably seen as a time-saving exercise. Clearly it took the company some time to realise that through-body stringing is one of the factors that makes a Tele sound like a Tele, but within a year or so they were thankfully back to the original method.

During all the changes and additions to the Fender line in its first decade, visually the humble Telecaster had stayed largely the same. As we've seen, cosmetic alterations had included a change from the original black to a white pickguard in late 1954. But otherwise the Telecaster looked pretty much the same blond-finished guitar it had been in 1951.

In 1959, however, two new models joined the Fender line that gave a quite different look when compared to the regular blond Telecaster and Esquire. These two new arrivals were the Custom Telecaster and the Custom Esquire. Each had a sunburst-finish body with bound edges. Binding is the technique used to create a thin white strip on the edge of a guitar body, just as you would see regularly on acoustic flat-tops and other hollow-body instruments.

A FENDER CUSTOM COLOR, ESPECIALLY AN EARLY TELECASTER, IS A PRIME CATCH. SO HOW MUCH IS A COAT OF PAINT WORTH?

Factory boss Forrest White had acquired some valuable advice on the process of binding from Fred Martin, head of the leading American flat-top acoustic guitar

Green onions & Bakersfield twang

1963 Fender Custom Telecaster

The Custom Telecaster and Esquire models, launched by Fender in 1959, had a quite different look, finished in the sunburst style of the Stratocaster and with bound white edges to the bodies. The Custom Telecaster pictured has the three-tone sunburst of the period, while the binding is clearly visible in this period ad (far left). The original Custom Esquire would last in the company's lines until 1969, the Tele for three years longer. Meanwhile, a host of players were discovering the tone and playability of the classic Telecaster, few to more impressive effect than Steve Cropper (opposite) whose economically graceful lines were heard on Stax sessions, not least Booker T's memorable 'Green Onions'. A driving, twangier sound came from Bakersfield, California, in the 1960s, led by Buck Owens and his Buckaroos guitarist Don Rich, pictured onstage (above) with their custom-made sparkle-finish Teles.

manufacturer, Martin. "I said Fred, I'd like to put binding around a Telecaster but I don't know a darned thing about it. He showed me how they cut the binding material, bought in sheets and cut into strips, and what kind of adhesive to use."[44]

The Customs were launched at the summer 1959 NAMM show in New York City. Fender's press release described them as "improved models" and "extremely attractive instruments", noting retail prices of $194.50 for the Esquire Custom and $229.50 for the Telecaster Custom, each $30 more than the regular unbound blond versions.

The new Customs also had rosewood fingerboards, as on the Jazzmaster, Fender's new top-of-the-line electric introduced the previous year. During 1959 the new separate rosewood fingerboard on a maple neck was adopted for all Fender models, including regular Telecasters and Esquires. It replaced Fender's previous construction that slid frets directly into the solid maple neck. Some players like the smooth, slippery style of maple, while others prefer the more textured feel of rosewood. Maple remained as an option at various times following the introduction of rosewood.

As Fender entered the 1960s, the company boasted apparently ever-extending lines of products. By July 1962 the pricelist included nine electric models (Duo-Sonic, Esquire, Esquire Custom, new-for-'62 Jaguar, Jazzmaster, Musicmaster, Stratocaster, Telecaster, and Telecaster Custom) and three basses (Precision Bass, Jazz Bass, and VI). There were 13 amplifiers (Bandmaster, Bassman, Champ, Concert, Deluxe, Princeton, Pro Amp, Showman, Super, Tremolux, Twin Amp, Vibrasonic, and Vibrolux). Completing the line-up were five steel guitars (Champ, Deluxe, Dual, Stringmaster, and Studio Deluxe) and two pedal steel guitars (400 and 1000).

The Vibrasonic had introduced some new amp features to the line in 1959: it had a new style of cabinet with a sloping, front-mounted control panel, and was finished in a hard-wearing vinyl material, Tolex, that now replaced Fender's classic 'tweed' linen covering on all amps. A new kind of set-up was introduced in 1961, the 'piggyback' Showman rig. This had the electronics housed in a separate box sitting on top of the separate speaker cabinet: a familiar arrangement now, but new at the time. Also new to the 1961 Fender line was reverberation ('reverb'), an effect created with a vibrating spring. It was first seen in the separate Fender Reverb unit, but shortly made its way into amps such as the Vibroverb.

At $379.50 the Jaguar was Fender's new top-of-the-line electric, with its shorter 24-inch-scale neck a come-on to Gibson players. It shared the novel offset-waist body shape that the Jazzmaster had introduced. It also had the Jazzmaster's separate bridge and vibrato unit, although the Jaguar had the addition of a (generally avoided) spring-loaded string mute at the bridge. The Jag had relatively complex controls, too. Like the Jazzmaster it had two separate volume and tone control circuits that the player could preset and select with the small slide-switch above the neck pickup. It added three selectors below the neck pickup that provided a tone switch and two pickup on/offs.

All this could not have been in greater contrast to the still gloriously simple Telecaster and Esquire. And these straightforward guitars were finding a true voice in the hands of similarly uncomplicated yet accomplished musicians. In the Stax studio in Memphis, cool-hand Steve Cropper translated the good old Telecaster's simplicity of design into musical terms as his lean guitar lines graced the 1962 Booker T & the MGs hit, 'Green Onions'. Cropper created a new classic Tele look, opting for the more recent style of blond body, white 'guard, and rosewood neck.

Listen a little later, too, for Cropper's beautifully measured opening statement and supporting licks on Sam & Dave's 'Soul Man' hit of 1967 and his contributions to Otis Redding's 'Dock Of The Bay', added to the basic track almost immediately following Redding's premature death in '67.

Rich, Nichols, and the Bakersfield twang

A new sound emerging in the early 1960s has become known variously as Bakersfield, because that was the California city, 100 miles to the north of Los Angeles, where it started, or Nashville West, because it was a peculiarly west-coast version of country music. Whatever the description, the key guitarist in this danceable music based on deep, driving electric guitars was Don Rich. He played with Buck Owens & The Buckaroos, first on fiddle and from 1962 on guitar. Owens, a fine Tele player himself, was named country music artist of the 1960s by Capitol Records, and with good reason: he and the band scored a remarkable 19 country-chart Number 1s during the decade.

Rich drew a cutting sound from his Telecaster, virtually inventing the idea that the Tele was the perfect machine for such a noise. Cock an ear to his bassy rhythm and chicken-pickin' breaks on Owens hits like 1963's 'Act Naturally', soon covered by The Beatles, who were big fans of this kind of incisive guitar twang. Two of the most famous Teles of the time were the sparkle-finish models custom-made for Rich and Owens, a pair of guitars that dazzled many an audience for the Bakersfield outfit. Rich died at the age of just 32 in 1974, following a motorcycle accident.

Another key Bakersfield player was Roy Nichols – also a Telecaster man – who played with Merle Haggard's group The Strangers, formed in the mid 1960s. James Burton played on some of these tracks, but it's probably Nichols supplying the demure but definitive chicken-pickin' that decorates Haggard's 1967 hit 'The Fugitive' (later renamed 'I'm A Lonesome Fugitive'). Nichols, who died in 2001, is buried at Greenlawn Cemetery in Bakersfield, and pictured on his gravestone is a guitar. It is, of course, a Telecaster.

The chicken-pickin' that Rich and Burton and Nichols introduced to record buyers' ears was a technique based on rapid-fire picking with a muted string click followed by a clean note, and so on around and around. The stuttering result sounds something like a clucking chicken – hence the name – and is so well suited to the dry attack of a Telecaster that it has become almost entirely associated with the instrument.

In the meantime, Fender had found itself in the midst of the rock'n'roll revolution of the late 1950s and early 1960s – and was happy to ensure that players had a good supply of affordable guitars available in large numbers. In a relatively short period the brilliantly inventive trio of Telecaster, Precision Bass and Stratocaster had combined to establish in

Shake your money maker

▲ 1960 Fender Telecaster fiesta red

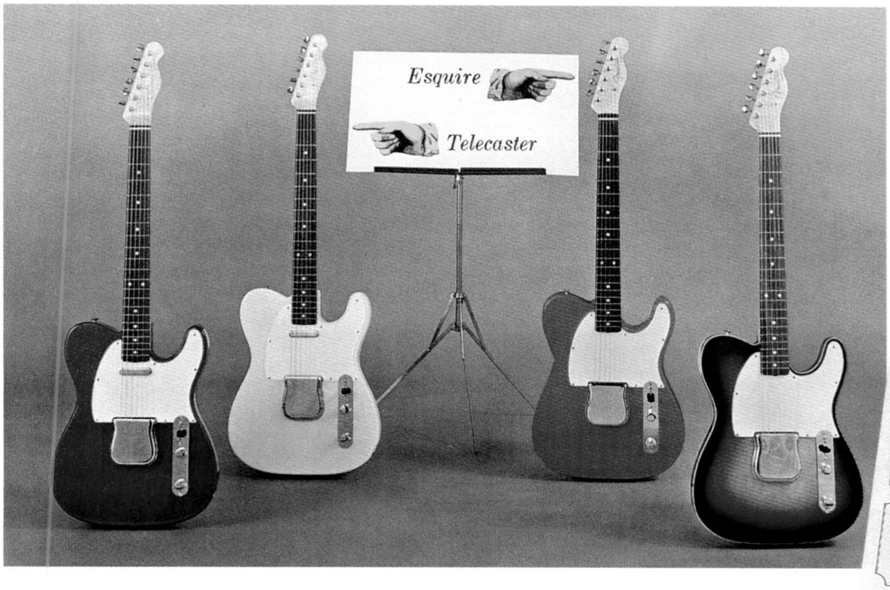

Mike Bloomfield is captured on film with his cutting Tele onstage with the Butterfield Blues Band (left) at the 1965 Newport festival. At the same event Bloomfield played with Bob Dylan, famously bringing Fender electricity to acoustic folk. Fender's 1963-64 catalogue (above) illustrated (far left) a rare 'red-mahogany' option, with see-through red finish on mahogany body. The company's 1965/66 catalogue (below) featured a regular blond ash-body Esquire, the red-mahogany Tele again, and a sunburst Custom Tele. Meanwhile, in the UK Fender guitars had been unavailable throughout the 1950s because of a trade ban, but by 1960 at last a distributor had been appointed. In the mid 1960s Arbiter became the new British agent, hyping the Telecaster in an ad (above right) as the country's "most wanted guitar".

the minds of musicians and guitar-makers the idea of the solidbody electric guitar as a viable modern instrument. What is remarkable is that in these circumstances Fender got so much right, and nearly always the first time. In short, the company had become remarkably successful.

Exporting had also become important to Fender's huge success, and had started in 1960 when Randall first visited the leading European trade show at Frankfurt, Germany. "Our products were known over there because of the GIs playing our guitars," he recalled, "and they were very much prized. So we started doing business in Europe." Britain became an especially important market in the 1960s because of the worldwide success of its pop groups. Up to the start of the 1960s it had been virtually impossible for British musicians to buy Fenders, because from 1951 to 1959 there was a government ban on importing American merchandise.

In 1960 Jennings became the first official British distributor of Fender gear, joined by Selmer in 1962. A Jennings pricelist from 1961 pitches the Telecaster at £107/9s/7d (£107.48, about $300 at the time); three years later the Tele had crept up to £122/17/0 (£122.85). By summer 1965, both Selmer and Jennings had been replaced as the British Fender distributor by Arbiter, who would continue for many years as the brand's U.K. agent. "Fender was the biggest musical instrument exporter in the United States," said Randall. "In fact I think we exported more U.S.-made musical products than all the other companies combined. We had it to ourselves for maybe three or four years."[45] Western Europe was the biggest export market, but Fender also did well in Scandinavia, South Africa, Rhodesia (now Zimbabwe), Japan, Australia, Canada, and elsewhere.

Fender commanded a huge segment of the new market. Many buildings had been added to cope with increased manufacturing demands, and by 1964 the operation employed some 600 people (500 in manufacturing) spread over 29 buildings. Forrest White said his guitar production staff were making 1,500 instruments a week at the end of 1964, compared to the 40 a week Fender had been making when he joined the company ten years earlier. As well as electric guitars, Fender's pricelist in 1964 offered amplifiers, steel guitars, electric basses, acoustic guitars, effects units, a host of related accessories, and Fender-Rhodes electric pianos, added to the line the previous year.

Don Randall remembered writing a million dollars' worth of sales during his first year in the 1950s, which rose to some ten million dollars' worth in the mid 1960s, translating to about $40 million of retail sales. By now the beat boom, triggered by The Beatles and the so-called British Invasion of pop groups, was taking the United States by storm. Electric guitars were at their peak of popularity, and Fender was among the biggest and most successful producers.

Time to meet the new boss

In January 1965 the Fender companies were sold to the mighty Columbia Broadcasting System Inc, better known as CBS. *The Music Trades* magazine reported in somewhat shocked tones: "The purchase price of $13 million is by far the highest ever offered in the history of the [musical instrument] industry for any single manufacturer. ... The acquisition, a sterling proof of the music industry's growth potential, marks the first time that one of the nation's largest corporations has entered our field. With sales volume in excess of half a billion dollars annually, CBS currently does more business than the entire [U.S. musical instrument] industry does at retail. Actual purchase of Fender was made by the Columbia Records Distribution Division of CBS, whose outstanding recent feats have included the production of *My Fair Lady*."[46]

Economic analysts were advising big corporations to diversify and acquire companies from a variety of different businesses. They were doubtless told that all they had to do was finance and expand the new acquisitions, and rich pickings would follow. Columbia Records boss Goddard Lieberson said of Fender: "This is a fast growing business tied into the expanding leisure time market. We expect this industry to grow by 23 per cent in the next two years."[47]

Leo Fender was by all accounts a hypochondriac, and the sale of Fender was prompted by his acute worries about his health, principally the staph infection in his sinuses that had troubled him since the mid 1950s. Also, he was nervous about financing expansion. He recalled later: "I thought I was going to have to retire. I had been suffering for years with a virus infection of the sinuses and it made my life a misery. I felt that I wasn't going to be in the health to carry on."[48]

"I CALLED LEO AND SAID HOW DOES THAT SUIT YOU? HE SAID OH, I CAN'T BELIEVE IT, ARE YOU TRYING TO PULL MY LEG?"

Don Randall tells Leo Fender they've just made $13 million

The sale of Fender to CBS was handled by Don Randall, who said that Leo had earlier offered him the company for a million-and-a-half dollars. Randall didn't feel he was ready for that kind of career move, so suggested to Leo that he might see what he could get from an outside buyer. Leo agreed, and Randall's first tentative discussions took place in early 1964 with the Baldwin Piano & Organ Co of Ohio. Randall also contacted an investment banker, who at first suggested that Fender go public, which neither Leo nor Randall wished to pursue. The bankers then came up with CBS as a potential purchaser.

"Now we had two companies up there," Randall remembered, "but Baldwin's attitude to purchasing turned out to be totally unsatisfactory for our purposes. So finally we got down to the nitty gritty with Columbia, and I made about half a dozen trips back and forth to New York: jam sessions with attorneys and financial people.

"The guys at CBS came in with a really low price at first, but eventually we came to a fairly agreeable price, and I called Leo and said how does that suit you? He said oh Don, I can't believe it, are you trying to pull my leg? And I said no – does that sound like a satisfactory deal we can close on? 'Well anything you say Don, that's fine, you just go ahead and do it,' he said. And so the rest is history, we went on and sold it to CBS after

Talking 'bout the CBS generation

Pete Townshend may have been more associated with Rickenbacker guitars in the 1960s, but in the middle of the decade he took up a Telecaster. Our Who picture (opposite) clearly shows that he had an extra pickup added to give something like a Stratocaster layout. Some players did modify the Tele's electrics, most often the 'weaker' front pickup, and the idea became more widespread in the 1970s. But the 1960s were a time of great upheaval for the Fender operation, which in 1965 was sold to the vast and powerful CBS corporation for $13 million, an unprecedented figure in the musical instrument industry. There has been a great deal of debate ever since about the way the new owners acted to affect the quality of Fender guitars. But whatever the changes, Telecasters continued to pour from the factory, and as ever the coloured-finish instruments remained in the minority. Two 'post-CBS' examples are pictured here, one with the newly available maple-fingerboard option.

▸ **1969 Fender Telecaster candy apple red**

▸ **1967 Fender Telecaster sherwood green**

a lot of investigation. They did a big study on us – people came in to justify the sale and the price paid – and we consummated the deal. Leo wouldn't even go back to New York for the signing, for the pay-off or anything. 'You get the money and you bring it out to me,' he said."[49]

In the year following the Fender acquisition, CBS published a survey that estimated the number of guitar players in the U.S. at nine million and placed total American retail sales of guitars during 1965 at $185 million, up from $24 million in 1958. CBS were clearly enthusiastic about the potential for music, and went on to buy more instrument companies such as Rogers (drums), Steinway (pianos), and Leslie (organ loudspeakers).

Creating Better Stuff or Causing Bitter Strife?

Over the years, the sale of Fender to CBS provoked much retrospective consternation among guitar players and collectors, some of whom consider so-called 'pre-CBS' instruments – in other words those made prior to the beginning of 1965 – as superior to those made after that date. This is of course a meaningless generalisation, but there can be little doubt that over a period of time after the sale, CBS did introduce changes to the production methods of Fender guitars, and that a number of these changes were detrimental to the quality of some instruments. According to some insiders, the problem with CBS at this time was that they seemed to believe that it was enough simply to pour lots of money into Fender. And certainly Fender's sales did increase and profits did go up – Randall recalled income almost doubling in the first year that CBS owned Fender. Profit became paramount, said Forrest White, who remained as manager of electric guitar and amplifier production. "CBS had a vice president for everything. I think they had a vice president for cleaning the toilets. You name it, whatever it was, it had a vice president."[50]

"CBS WERE AS INTERESTED IN QUALITY AS WE WERE AND SPARED NO EFFORT TO ENSURE QUALITY WAS THERE."
Don Randall on the new owners

Here was a significant clash of cultures. The new CBS men, often trained engineers with college degrees, believed in high-volume production. Fender's old guard were long-serving craft workers without formal qualifications. A job ad in the *Los Angeles Times* in March 1966 summed up the changes. It was for a Systems Analyst to oversee a computer feasibility study at Fender, for a "management information system" covering "sales order processing, material control, manufacturing systems, and accounting systems". It's not hard to imagine the rumours that this probably set in motion among the old team. They want to run the place with computers! Whatever next!

Among the old-guard Fender men who talked to us for this book, opinion about the effect of the CBS takeover on Fender's guitars seemed divided. George Fullerton said that management were first alerted to criticisms when complaints started to filter back from the dealers through the sales reps. "They'd say the guitars don't play like they used to, they aren't adjusted like they used to be," said Fullerton.[51] Salesman Dale Hyatt reckoned that the quality of Fender instruments stayed relatively stable until around 1968, and then quality control declined. "It got to the point where I did not enjoy going to any store anywhere," Hyatt recalled, "because every time I walked in I found myself defending some poor piece of workmanship. They got very sloppy with the finish, with far too many bad spots, and the neck sockets were being cut way over size. They blamed that on the new three-bolt neck but it wasn't that – put six bolts in it and it still would have moved. And they created their own competition, letting the door wide open for everybody else, including the Japanese."[52]

Randall, who under the new owners became vice president and general manager of Fender Musical Instruments and Fender Sales (both soon part of the new CBS Musical Instruments Division), thought the supposition that quality deteriorated when CBS took over is a fallacy. "I will say this for CBS, they were just as interested in quality as we were. They spared no amount of time or effort to ensure the quality was there. There's always this suspicion when a big company takes over that they're going to make a lousy product and sell it for a higher price, and that's not true here. But the other problems that existed were multiple."[53]

Leo's services were retained as "special consultant in research and development". CBS's confidential pre-sale report into the Fender operation had concluded that Leo, unlike Randall, was not a necessity to running the business, and that while "a competent chief engineer" could easily keep products moving forward in the contemporary marketplace, it would be "highly desirable, at least for a period of four or five years, to maintain the active interest and creativity of Mr Fender".[54] In other words, CBS didn't want Leo taking his ideas elsewhere, but didn't particularly want him getting in the way of the newly efficient Fender business machine. So he was set up away from the Fender buildings, allowed to tinker as much as he liked – with very little effect on the product.

A couple of years after the sale to CBS, Leo changed doctors and was given a massive dose of antibiotics that cured his sinus complaint. He completed a few projects for CBS but left when his five-year contract expired in 1970. He went on to make instruments for the Music Man company (originally set up in 1972 although not named Music Man until 1974) and his later G&L operation, where the ASAT model was more or less a Telecaster with a different name.

Leo had not been the first of the old guard to leave CBS. Forrest White departed in 1967 "because I wouldn't build some products – the solid state amps – that I thought were unworthy of Leo's name",[55] and went on to work with Leo at Music Man, as well as for CMI (which owned Gibson) and Rickenbacker. White died in November 1994. Don Randall resigned from CBS in April 1969, disenchanted with corporate life, and formed Randall Electric Instruments, which he sold in 1987. George Fullerton left CBS in 1970, worked at Ernie Ball for a while, and with Leo formed the G&L company in 1979, although Fullerton sold his interest in 1986. (G&L at first stood for "George & Leo", later "Guitars by Leo".) Dale Hyatt, who resigned from CBS in 1972, was also part of the G&L set-up, which

Set the controls for some groovy naturals

▲ **1968 Fender Thinline Telecaster**

The 1960s proved a good time for British guitarists with Teles in tow, and fans looked no further than The Yardbirds for a run of great Fender men. Eric Clapton (opposite, left) often played a red Telecaster in the group, which upon leaving he passed to Jeff Beck (opposite, right). The new boy disliked the hand-me-down and quickly acquired his own weapons: an enviable and effective pair of Esquire and Telecaster. Syd Barrett (left) had a much more impressionistic role in mind for his Tele amid the psychedelic ramblings of Pink Floyd. Fender meanwhile decided to bring some acoustic tone to the Tele and launched the Thinline model in 1968 (main guitar), complete with hollowed-out body 'pockets' and a token f-hole. As well as the sunburst finish pictured, the Thinline came in what Fender's 1968 ad (above) called "groovy natural" ash or mahogany.

was sold to BBE Sound Inc after Leo Fender's death in March 1991 at the age of 82.

One of Fender's first CBS-era pricelists, dated April 1965, revealed a burgeoning line of products. A regular Telecaster cost $209.50 and an Esquire $169.50; bound Custom versions were $30 more. There were seven more electric guitar models: Duo-Sonic, Electric XII, Jaguar, Jazzmaster, Musicmaster, Mustang, Stratocaster. The other lines included three bass guitars (Jazz, Precision, VI), six flat-top acoustics (Classic, Concert, King, Malibu, Palomino, Newporter) and 15 amplifiers (Bandmaster, Bassman, Champ, Deluxe, Deluxe Reverb, Dual Showman, Princeton, Princeton Reverb, Pro Reverb, Showman, Super Reverb, Tremolux, Twin Reverb, Vibro Champ, Vibrolux Reverb), as well as various Fender-Rhodes keyboards, steel and pedal steel guitars, a solidbody electric mandolin, and reverb and echo units.

Back around 1960 Fender had started to use a modernised 'chunky' Fender logo in company literature. The first electric to brandish the new design on its headstock was the 1962 Jaguar. During the following years Fender gradually applied it to all guitars, though it didn't arrive on the Telecaster until about 1966. This new logo, drawn up by adman Bob Perine, is known now among collectors as the 'transition' logo, because it leads from the original thin 'spaghetti' logo to a bolder black version introduced around 1968. In 1965 Fender began to stamp the modernised 'F' of the new logo on to guitar neck-plates and, shortly after, on to new-design tuners.

"IT'S BEEN PAINTED SEVERAL TIMES, AND ONCE I EVEN COVERED IT IN PLASTIC SHEETING AND SILVER DISCS."
Syd Barrett on his shiny Tele

During 1966 CBS completed the construction of a new Fender factory (planned before their purchase of the company) at a cost of $1.3 million. It was situated next to Fender's existing buildings on the South Raymond site. Clearly the new owners were getting ready for a real push on production. CBS didn't have much cause for concern in terms of demand.

Pop music was, of course, flourishing in the 1960s – and Telecasters were everywhere. Mike Bloomfield turned up with one for an apparently casual Bob Dylan performance at the Newport folk festival in July 1965, introducing an audience more used to acoustic guitars to the capabilities of a turned-up Tele. A month earlier Bloomfield had played his Tele on the recording of 'Like A Rolling Stone'. The following year Robbie Robertson too toted a Tele when The Hawks backed Dylan for a series of now legendary live shows that further staked out the ground occupied by folk-rock.

In Britain, despite strong competition during this heady decade from the Gibson Les Paul and the Stratocaster among pro players, the Telecaster held its own. An early boost came with Mick Green in Johnny Kidd & The Pirates, notably on hits such as 'I'll Never Get Over You' (1963) where Green's deft mix of chords and single-line work benefited from the Tele's cutting sound. In 1965 Pete Townshend, well known for on-stage guitar destruction, briefly favoured a Tele, telling an interviewer that it was the "toughest guitar".

The journalist agreed, revealing a less well-known attribute of the instrument: "The final proof came when he whacked it against an 18-inch-thick pillar, chipping the concrete but only bruising the guitar."[56]

As psychedelia loomed, Syd Barrett of Pink Floyd was setting the controls of his Telecaster for a series of long, experimental work-outs. Barrett exploited the Tele's potential for noise and sound effects as well as its more customary sonic values. He used a typical rosewood-board Tele of the time, probably bought new around 1964. "It's been painted several times, and once I even covered it in plastic sheeting and silver discs," Barrett said in 1967. "Those discs are still on the guitar, but they tend to look a bit worn."[57]

"WHY A TELE? BECAUSE OF THE SOUND OF RICKY NELSON'S RECORDS. WHEN WE PLUGGED IN OUR TELE, IT SOUNDED A LOT LIKE JAMES BURTON."
Jeff Beck recalls early influences

Jimi Hendrix was the quintessential Strat player, but his sound wizard Roger Mayer has recalled that a couple of classic solos were recorded on a Tele. Mayer had been building Jimi a new effects unit, the Octavia frequency-doubler. Early in 1967 there was a plan to try the new unit at a recording session following a gig. At the evening's show, said Mayer, "Jimi had a Strat with him and put it through the ceiling, bashing up the tuners. So when we went to Olympic studio later that night to do some overdubs using the Octavia, Jimi had to send [bassist] Noel Redding out to get a Telecaster. He used it for the overdubs to 'Fire' and 'Purple Haze', including the Octavia solo on 'Purple Haze'."[58] Other Brits valued the Tele's worth, and 1968 proved a good year: Justin Hayward of The Moody Blues played some great Tele licks on the 'Ride My See-Saw' single, and Davy O'List wrestled howling, squealing solos from his Tele's neck pickup on The Nice's Top 10 hit 'America'.

Just before Eric Clapton left The Yardbirds he had been playing a red Telecaster, owned by the group's management. Jeff Beck inherited the guitar briefly when he replaced Clapton in February 1965. "I had to use that because I didn't have a guitar when I joined," Beck recalled. "I'd already sold my first Fender, a Strat, but I got rid of the red Tele soon after. It was a terrible guitar. John Owen, the rhythm guitarist in my previous group, The Tridents, had a Telecaster. I would ogle this thing, and I spent more time playing it than he did. Then I borrowed it – and I never gave it back."

Beyond the brief red Tele, it was Owen's blond '59 or '60 rosewood-neck Tele that Beck used at first in The Yardbirds. But why did he want a Telecaster? "Because of the sound that Ricky Nelson's records had. We all thought that was a Telecaster. We weren't sure, because there was no information on the records at all. I don't know who told us, but we all assumed it was a Tele because it sounded so close when we plugged in our one: on the back pickup it sounded a lot like James Burton.

"And then I saw that film *The Girl Can't Help It* at the Sutton Granada, after school, in May or June of '56. It was the most pivotal film in my career, and my life, really." Beck

Stairway to Bigsby

▲ **1969 Fender Telecaster blue ice metallic**

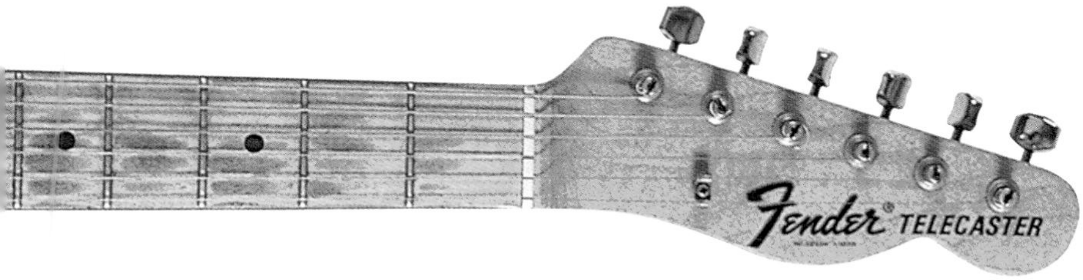

▲ **1968 Fender Telecaster**

Completing the full set of ex-Yardbirds Tele guitarists, Jimmy Page (opposite) plays the guitar Jeff Beck gave him, with Page's added decoration. Later in Led Zeppelin Page would use the same Tele for his iconic 'Stairway To Heaven' solo. From 1968 Fender began to offer the option of a factory-fitted Bigsby vibrato, as seen in the catalogue from that year (above) and the two late-1960s Teles shown here. The 1969 example was finished in blue ice metallic, but as often happens the lacquer top coat has yellowed with age to give this attractive, mellow green colour.

watched slack-jawed as Little Richard's band performed. There in the background was a chap with a lovely battered maple-neck black-'guard Tele. "It was just mouth-watering for us!" Then on came Gene Vincent & His Blue Caps. Beck knew that Cliff Gallup played guitar with this lot – and there on film was a 15-year-old blond kid playing an Esquire. Must be Gallup, he concluded. Turned out it was a stand-in, one Russell Willaford. "He remains a massive mystery," Beck recalled. "No one ever found out anything about the guy; he just came and did the film and disappeared, and did some publicity shots – with an Esquire."

Fast forward to April 1965, and Beck got an Esquire to use alongside his 'borrowed' Tele in The Yardbirds. His *Girl Can't Help It* guitars were complete. "I bought my first Esquire from John Walker," he said. The Yardbirds were put on a Kinks package tour, but The Kinks pulled out after an on-stage brawl and were replaced by The Walker Brothers. "First thing I saw at rehearsals was this really good-looking pair of brothers, and one had an Esquire with a white pickguard and blond neck – and I wanted that blond neck. You couldn't get the blond neck after a certain run, they changed it to rosewood. I said I want that guitar! He said oh, 75 quid then. Give over! They're only about 85 quid new! And his had been shaved into a contoured body. I bought it anyway."

Beck made his great series of Yardbirds recordings, each one an object lesson in the inventive, experimental use of electric guitar on bluesy-pop records. 'Heart Full Of Soul' was the Tele; 'Shapes Of Things' the Esquire. But surely it couldn't have been easy to persuade the Esquire to feed back for 'Shapes'? "That was done in Chess Records," remembered Beck, "where we were all completely blown away with the way they did things. The drum sound was great, and everything was like a dream come true – because we were playing in Chess, albeit the last throes of it. Marshall Chess was there and the guys that used to record Muddy; really great. I was standing right next to an AC-30 on a chair, which I used so that I could easily reach the controls. I just moved around to get the right noise, you know? It was madness, pure experimentation.

"I wanted a Les Paul, but when I got it, it was so refined, and not really the tool you need on stage for some reason. The controls were in the wrong place: I kept hitting the pickup selector on/off into the wrong position. But the Esquire was no problem at all. I used to spin it around on top of the amp and change the speed of the echo while it was feeding back. Total lunacy! I used to try and break it – and I never broke it."

When he left The Yardbirds at the end of 1966, Beck passed on the Telecaster to Jimmy Page, by now the group's other guitar player. "I left The Yardbirds in a huff," said Beck, "I just decided in a minute I was going to leave. So I didn't take the guitar, and Jimmy carried on playing. Because he was now the only lead guitarist, he had to mimic what I did, and that's how come he got the guitar. Jimmy plastered it with psychedelic paint, and all the early Zeppelin stuff was done on that, on John Owen's Telecaster."[59] We'll discover the fate of Beck's Yardbirds Esquire a little later.

Over in California, a change was made to the control wiring of the Tele around 1967, altering the circuit that had been used since about 1952. Now, the guitar operated pretty much as you'd expect from a two-pickup guitar: selector in the rear position gave bridge pickup only; the middle position switched in both pickups; and moving the selector to the front position gave the neck pickup only. The tone control worked with all combinations. Also starting this year, a Fender/Bigsby vibrato was offered as an optional extra on Teles and Esquires, lasting to about 1974.

Fender were still well known for excellent tube amplifiers, but issued their first Solid State (transistor) amps in 1967 – many of which quickly came back as unworkable. It was one of the first signs that CBS might not be acting in the best interests of the many musicians who relied on Fender products. At the same time, it had become obvious to management at CBS/Fender that the company's recent experiments with hollow-body guitars – a line of flat-tops, the electric thinline Coronados, and the full-body Montego and LTD models – were not a success. Most had by now been quietly dropped from the line.

A Tele with some air inside

Nonetheless Fender pressed forward with a new plan intended to gain some ground from rivals, primarily Gibson, who were dominating hollow-body electrics. This time, they took the Telecaster and produced a lighter version, the Thinline, beginning in 1968.

The new model was designed by Roger Rossmeisl and Virgilio 'Babe' Simoni, Fender's product manager of stringed instruments. Rossmeisl had been brought into the company by Leo in 1962 to design those (unsuccessful) hollow-body guitars. He was the son of a German guitar-maker and had come to the States in the 1950s, at first working for Gibson in Michigan but soon moving to Rickenbacker in California where he made a number of one-off custom guitars and designed production models such as the stylish Rick 300-series guitars.

Rossmeisl's Telecaster Thinline had three hollowed-out cavities inside the body, made in his Rickenbacker style by taking a slice off the back, routing out the cavities, and then gluing the back in place. The guitar had a modified pickguard shaped to accommodate the single, token f-hole. At first it retained the regular Telecaster pickup layout, although as we'll see it gained a humbucker later.

Fender's press release of the time said: "[The] famous Telecaster guitar is now available in a semi-acoustic model with a choice of two natural wood finishes, mahogany or ash. The lightweight hollow-body guitar incorporates Fender's distinctive f-hole design and new styled pickguard. The polyester-finished maple neck comes equipped with special lightweight strings for fast playing action." The new Telecaster Thinline came in what a Fender ad called "groovy natural" finishes – in ash or mahogany – with a list price of $319.50, making it $90 more than a regular Tele.

Rossmeisl did not last much longer at Fender. George Fullerton echoed a general feeling when he said: "Roger was a marvellous designer and didn't become the person he should have been. I think he was his own worst enemy. Such a waste."[60] Rossmeisl died in Germany in 1979 at the age of 52.

It was around this time – and quite apart from Fender – that Byrds guitarist Clarence White and drummer Gene Parsons came up with their string-bending device. White's first

From Presley's Paisley to White's B-Bender

1968 Fender Paisley Red Telecaster

James Burton (opposite, centre) plays his famous Paisley Red Tele with Elvis, almost in danger of upstaging the King. Burton has been one of the most influential Tele men of all time. Two new gaudily decorated Fender finishes were launched for Esquires and Telecasters in 1968: Burton's Paisley Red or the marginally more restful Blue Flower, promoted in Fender flyers (below) as "pulsating with every beat". Unfortunately most players other than Burton were not impressed and the models did not last long on the Fender pricelist. Another strange idea was the B-Bender, devised by Byrds guitarist Clarence White and drummer Gene Parsons. White wanted a 'third hand' to help with complex string bends; Parsons came up with a system of levers and a spring inside a hacked Tele body (the back cover hides the work, right). Pulling down on the neck would raise the pitch of the B-string, giving the athletic guitarist pedal-steel-like bends within chords.

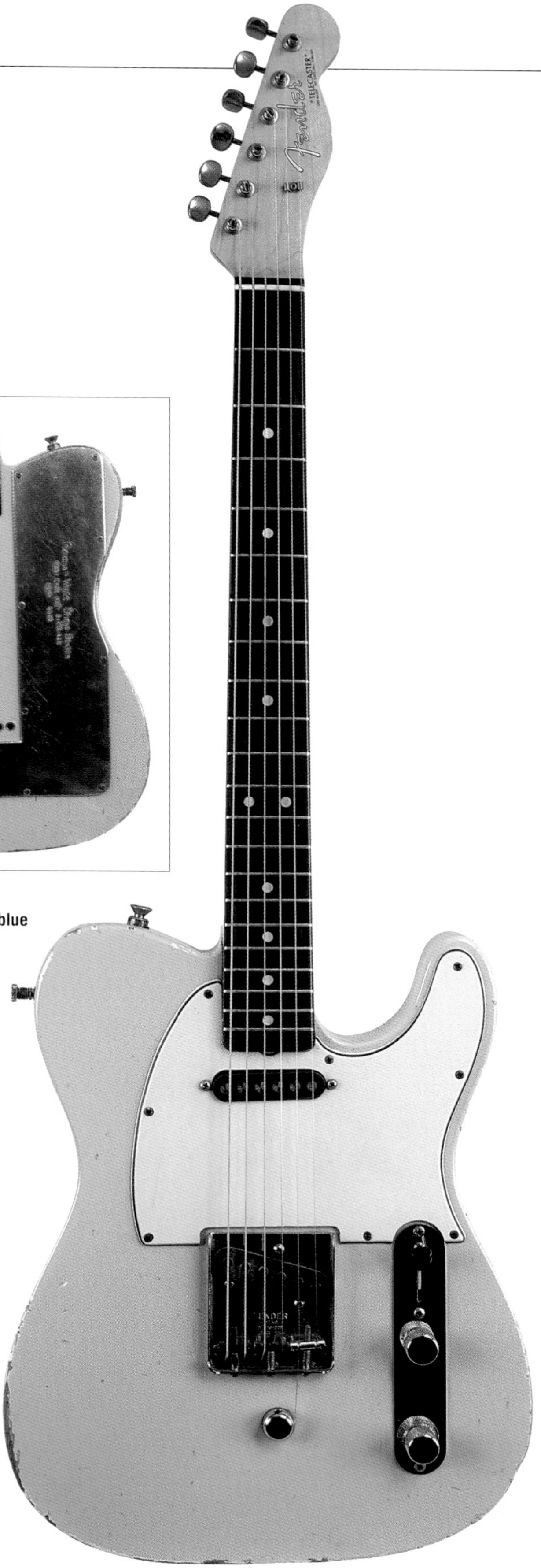

1964 Fender Telecaster sonic blue

FENDER'S
Blue Flower
Blue Flower bursts forth in a dazzling array of subtle purple and green patterns. Never before has such an exciting profusion of color been offered.
Telecaster $279.50, Telecaster Bass $289.50.
(These finishes are available on the Telecaster and Telecaster Bass only.)
Fender
MUSICAL INSTRUMENTS

electric band was Nashville West in 1967, where he moved from a Martin D-28 to a Tele, but it was at a Byrds session that he told Parsons about his need for a 'third hand' to help with some complicated string-bends he had in mind. Parsons obliged with the engineering, ingeniously controlled by a lever fitted inside a hacked Tele body and attached to the strap button on the top. Pulling down on the neck effectively raised the strap button – and shifted the lever plus some springs and rods inside – and raised the pitch of the B-string. Presto! String-bends within chords to emulate pedal steel-type sounds. Parsons and White applied for a patent for their B-bender in October 1968, granted 17 months later.

B-benders can be heard working away on only a select few records, as few guitarists have considered it worth the effort to master the necessary shoulder/arm co-ordination. But try listening to the co-inventor, Clarence White, injecting some carefully-positioned licks on 'Chestnut Mare' by The Byrds in 1970; Bernie Leadon bending the notes on 'Peaceful Easy Feeling' by The Eagles in 1972; or Jimmy Page shouldering a Tele on 'All My Love' from Led Zeppelin's last album together, 1979's *In Through The Out Door*.

Elvis eyes up Burton's Paisley Tele

In 1968 psychedelia hit Fender when they applied self-adhesive wallpaper with a paisley or floral pattern to some Telecasters, presumably in order to give them fresh flower-power appeal. Certainly the Paisley Red and Blue Flower Teles could not be described as examples of CBS's boring approach to guitar design. But the Tele seemed the least likely target for the creation of such far-out psychedelic art objects.

The Paisley Red quickly became identified with James Burton who, since we left him back in the late 1950s with Ricky Nelson, had played with scores if not hundreds of artists. But in 1969 he landed a plum gig with Elvis Presley, and would remain as Presley's guitarist until the singer's death in 1977.

"When I first went to work with Elvis I was playing my early-'50s Tele that my dad got me, the one I used on 'Suzie Q' and all the Ricky Nelson songs," said Burton. "In '69 the vice president of Fender, Chuck Weiner, called me and said I have a guitar here that has your name on it. I said really? Send it to me. He said no, I want you to come down and check it out. Come and have lunch. So I drove to Fullerton, went in his office – and he said it's over there, in the corner. I opened up the case and oh! It was shocking! Pink paisley! I said no, no, no, no. I said maybe a heavy rock'n'roll guitar player, not me. He said oh yeah, it's yours, take it. He was sure, his mind was made up, and he was not going to let me get out of there without the guitar. So I said OK, I'll take it.

"I took the guitar, and I decided well, maybe I'll take it to Vegas with me, check it out later. About two weeks into the Elvis Vegas show I decided to bring it out. I didn't know what Elvis was going to say on stage, I was nervous, but I thought I'd take my chance. So I took the guitar out, we're doing the first show, and he comes over to me, we're doing 'Johnny B Goode', and he's making like he's playing the guitar next to me. But he didn't say a word on stage.

"After the show, one of the Memphis Mafia guys comes down, Red West, says Elvis wants to see you in his dressing room. I go down and talk to him. He says, 'I notice you've got a different guitar tonight.' I said yeah. I told him the story about it, said I was a little nervous because maybe it was a little too flashy or something, didn't know how you'd accept that on stage. Oh, he said, I love it! Looks great, sounds great. Incredible! I had been so nervous! I thought he might say, Where d'you get that horrible guitar? But he loved it. He said, Man, it looks great.

"And this guitar had a sound, you know? It was different to my original Tele, a little fatter. I had my back pickup custom wound by a friend of mine, Red Rhodes. Hit that switch and the notes sound that big and round."[61] Much as it suited Burton – and he used the guitar not only with Presley but during his work with Emmylou Harris, Gram Parsons and many others – Fender's dazzling wallpaper experiment with the Paisley Red and Blue Flower Telecasters did not last long.

Meanwhile in amplifier land, some Fender models began to display a small cosmetic change from 1968, adopting a new aluminium control panel. These are now known among players and collectors as 'silverface' models to distinguish the colour of their control panels from the 'blackface' style that preceded them.

Alongside the amplifiers, speaker cabinets, effects units, electric pianos, organs, steel guitars, banjos, acoustics and all the rest on Fender's absolutely bursting 1968 pricelist were ten basic solidbody electrics: Bronco, Duo-Sonic, Esquire, Jaguar, Jazzmaster, Musicmaster, Mustang, Stratocaster, Telecaster, and 12-string.

Towards the end of the 1960s came firm evidence of CBS wringing every last drop of potential income from unused factory stock that would otherwise have been written off. Two shortlived guitars, called the Maverick (or Custom) and the Swinger, were cobbled from the leftovers. Fender's Dale Hyatt remembered the headaches that these concoctions caused him and his fellow salesmen. "They were abortions. Everybody knew what it was: a way to get rid of stuff. But people out there in the field are smarter than that. The dealers are smarter, they know. The musicians know better. But CBS didn't care, they made 'em and said here, you go sell 'em."[62]

FOR THE BEATLES' LAST EVER 'CONCERT', ON THE APPLE ROOFTOP, GEORGE HARRISON PLAYED A PROTOTYPE ROSEWOOD TELECASTER

And then there were The Beatles. As far as most casual onlookers were concerned, the group had nothing to do with Fender. In fact, George Harrison and John Lennon had each acquired a Stratocaster in 1965 for studio use, and Paul McCartney, increasingly confident with six rather than four strings, got himself an Esquire two years later, using it for his soaring, concise solo on *Sgt Pepper*'s 'Good Morning, Good Morning'. But the public image of the band remained distinctly Fender-less – leading Fender's Don Randall to try to persuade manager Brian Epstein to get his boys more visibly into the brand. "It

Shine until tomorrow

Fender sent George Harrison a prototype of an unusual rosewood-body Telecaster that the Beatle used for a good deal of the group's *Let It Be* movie and album. Harrison is pictured with the prototype (left) which he played most famously during The Beatles' last concert, filmed on the roof of their Apple HQ in London. Fender put the model into production in 1969 (main guitar) but the instrument's relatively heavy weight and unusual tonality meant it was a shortlived item in the catalogue. An ad from 1971 (opposite, bottom) revealed that Fender, like most people at the time, were unaware that the company's first solidbody had debuted in 1950. Changes to the 1970s line continued: the earlier f-hole Thinline model, with its single-coil pickups (late example, right, bottom), was altered in 1971 to incorporate two of Fender's new humbucking pickups (example shown right, top).

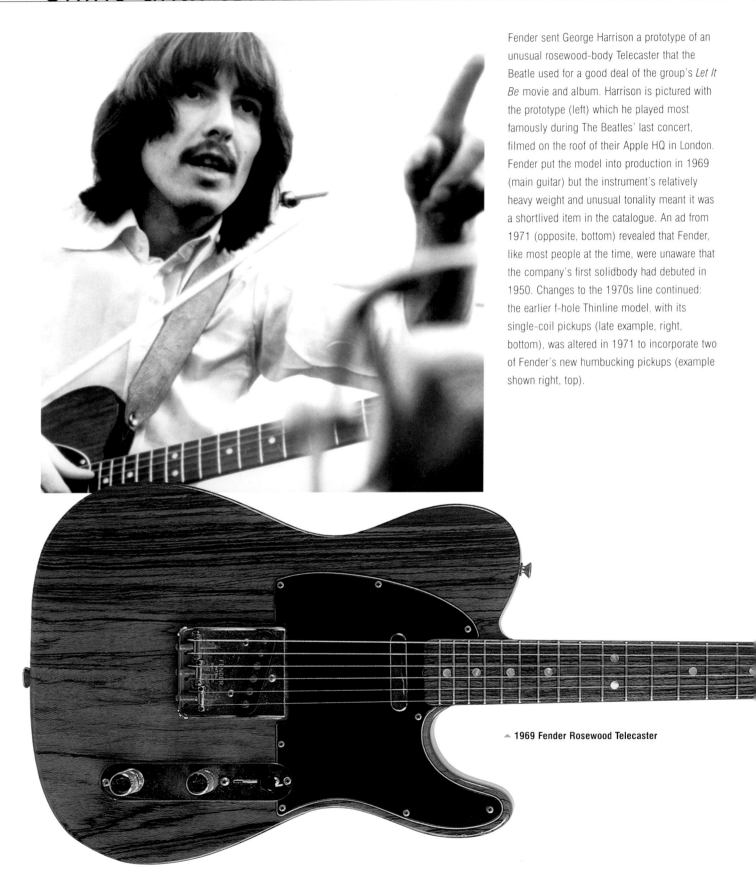

▲ **1969 Fender Rosewood Telecaster**

▲ 1972 Fender Thinline Telecaster sunburst

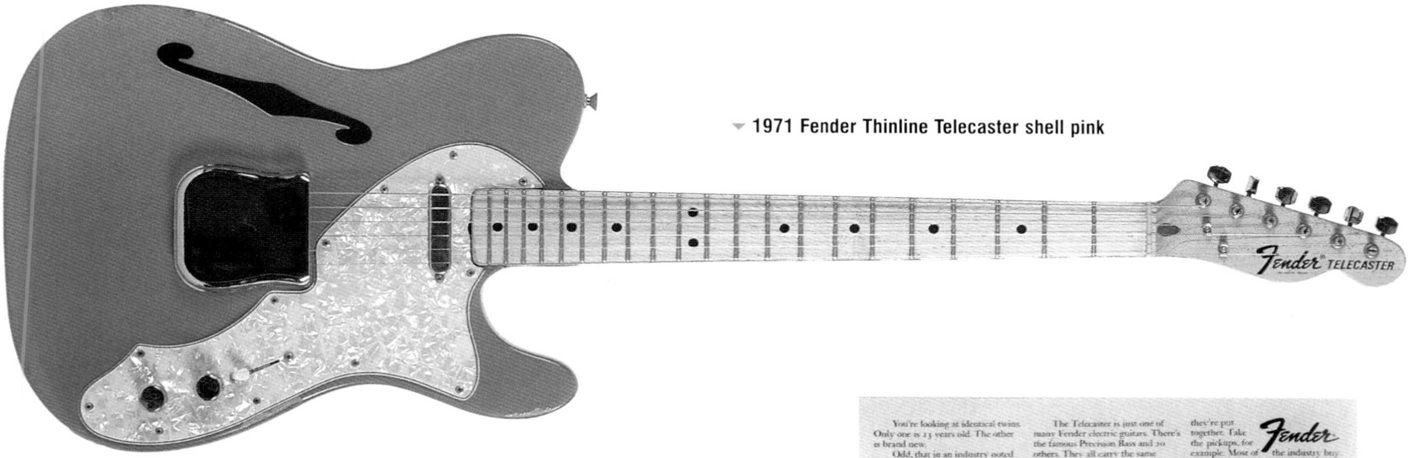

▼ 1971 Fender Thinline Telecaster shell pink

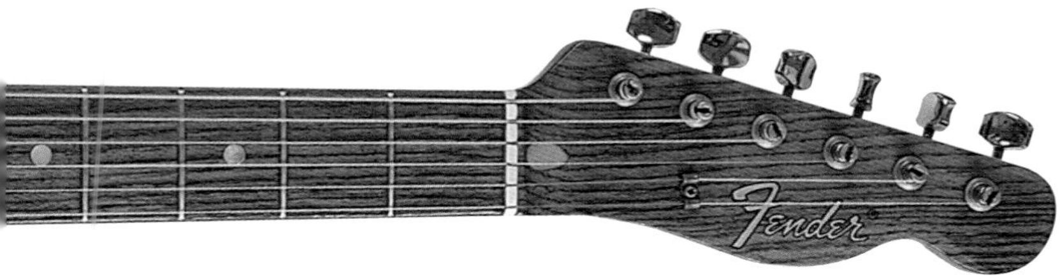

was the only time we ever tried to buy somebody off," Randall recalled. "I sent a member of my staff to try and buy Brian Epstein off. But no, it was a pittance."

In summer 1968, Randall managed to secure a meeting with Lennon and McCartney at the band's Apple headquarters in London. "I was still kind of interested in getting them to use our products. So we went up there and had quite a long conversation with Paul. He had some great ideas, a real animated guy. Finally John and Yoko came in, and we all sat down at this big conference table."[63] The results were the band's Fender-Rhodes pianos, a VI six-string bass, a Jazz Bass, a number of amps including a PA system, and Harrison's Rosewood Telecaster. From this point Fender's U.K. agent, Arbiter, supplied the group with more or less whatever they wanted.

The Beatles' last ever 'concert' was famously played on the rooftop of their Apple HQ in London in January 1969, featuring in the following year's movie *Let It Be* that effectively charted their break-up. On the roof and at other points during the making of the film and the accompanying album, Harrison played his Rosewood Telecaster, an unusual and shortlived model. Fender had sent one of the prototypes to Harrison in December 1968. They made two prototypes of the Rosewood Telecaster and two prototypes of a Rosewood Stratocaster, one of the latter intended for but never reaching Jimi Hendrix.

"I USE A WHOLE LOAD OF DIFFERENT GUITARS, THAT'S TRUE, BUT I MEAN, NINETY PERCENT ARE PROBABLY TELECASTERS, OLD ONES."
Keith Richards

The Rosewood Tele went into production later in 1969 and lasted a couple of years in the line. It had a body constructed from a thin layer of maple sandwiched between a solid rosewood top and back. It made for a striking yet heavy instrument. Fender attempted to lighten the load by moving to a two-piece construction with hollowed chambers inside, but the weight and unusual tonality meant it was never a popular instrument.

Some players and collectors believe that the 1970s are the poorest years of Fender's production history. Others who got their first instruments then are likely to have fonder memories. There's little doubt that quality control slipped and more low-standard Fenders were made during this decade than any other. But some fine Fender guitars were made in the 1970s as well. It's just that there were more average guitars made than good guitars, and it often seems as if the good ones were produced in spite rather than because of the company's policies and activities.

During the 1970s, CBS management cut back on the existing Fender product lines and offered hardly any new models. The last Esquires and Duo-Sonics of the period were made in 1969. George Fullerton recalled: "The powers that be also came up with the idea to drop the whole Telecaster line. And I just blew up! I went to Leo and I said no way, we will never, never, never drop this. I said, 'That's our beginning, that's our roots.' We'd have to be absolutely ashamed if we dropped that."[64] The Jaguar disappeared in 1975, and by

1980 the Bronco, Jazzmaster, Musicmaster, and Thinline Telecaster had all been phased out of production. Most were later reissued, but back in the day it made for a bare catalogue. Elsewhere in Fender's guitar lines the original acoustic flat-tops had all gone by 1971. Ten years later the steels and pedal steels had all disappeared, with only amplifiers (some 14 models) offering anything like the previous market coverage.

Make that one a humbucker

As far as the Telecaster was concerned, the 1970s might well be described as the decade of the humbucker. Part of Fender's distinction had come from using bright-sounding single-coil pickups; the warmer, fatter-sounding humbucking types were always seen then as a Gibson mainstay. Humbucking pickups had two coils wired in such a way that the noise often associated with single-coil pickups was cancelled. The bridge pickup on a Telecaster (or an Esquire) is widely praised as the heart of its sound, but the neck pickup ... well, that has often been seen by a good number of players as the instrument's weak link. Some guitarists simply didn't use it. Others took the matter into their own hands, or at least passed the problem on to their repairman.

A popular choice was to replace the mellow neck pickup with a ballsier humbucker, often lifted from a Gibson. Steve Marriott of The Small Faces gave this a try back at the time of the group's enjoyable *Ogden's Nut Gone Flake* album of 1968, but in the 1970s Keith Richards was the most visible user of a humbucker'd Tele. He was playing Teles regularly on stage with the Stones early in the decade, probably starting in 1972, even though he'd flirted with them live as early as 1966, and Brian Jones used a Tele to record his slide on 'Little Red Rooster' back in '64.

Keef's most famous Fender is his black-'guard 1950s Tele, nicknamed Micawber, complete with added Gibson humbucker. It's also one of the guitars he uses with five-string open tuning, effectively open G with the low D removed (G-D-G-B-D low to high), heard live on classics like 'Brown Sugar'. "I use a whole load of different guitars, that's true," he said in the early 1980s, "but they're not all that dissimilar in type. I mean, 90 percent are probably Telecasters, old ones."[65]

Denny Dias in Steely Dan went further and replaced both pickups of his Telecaster with humbuckers. Perhaps that means it's not really a Tele at all any more. No matter: Steely Dan made remarkable records in the 1970s, and on the first two albums Dias and Jeff Baxter provide some of the best and most exhilarating guitar playing of the decade. Dias solo'd less, but his highly modified Tele – a beast remodelled by Baxter with twin 'buckers, multiple coil switching, big frets, and a Strat bridge – can be heard on Dias's breathtaking, tumbling solo on 'Bodhisattva' from 1973's *Countdown To Ecstasy*.

In 1973 Jeff Beck exchanged his Yardbirds Esquire with Seymour Duncan for a custom Tele with humbuckers that the pickup maestro had put together. The 'Tele-Gib' combined a '59 Telecaster body, a '63/'64 neck, and a pair of Gibson humbuckers from a Flying V. "It had the feel of a Tele and just this big fat sound of the humbuckers," was Beck's summation. "It's a really good combination. Just doesn't look that great."

Two more ways to buck that hum

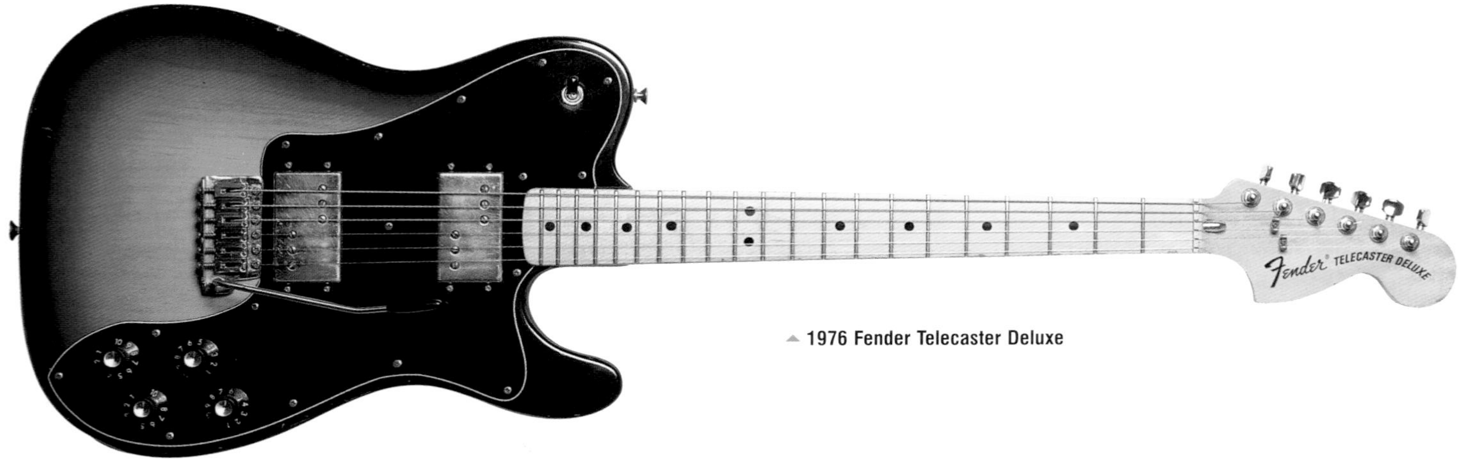

▲ 1976 Fender Telecaster Deluxe

▼ 1977 Fender Telecaster Custom

Two new Telecasters with Fender's humbucker pickups appeared in the early 1970s. The Telecaster Custom (main guitar) was in effect a regular Tele that acknowledged one of the most popular modifications that guitarists made to the instrument: replacing the 'weak' neck pickup with a ballsier humbucker. Fender also threw in a new-shape pickguard and a four-control layout. Keith Richards often used an old Telecaster with added neck 'bucker on-stage at the time but was also seen with one of the Customs (above). Another player keen on the humbucker'd Tele approach was Steely Dan's Denny Dias, pictured (above right) with his highly modified Tele in the early 1970s. The new Telecaster Deluxe (opposite, top) was similar to the Custom but had two humbuckers and a Stratocaster neck.

One of the finest moments for Beck's Tele-Gib came when he used it to record 'Cause We've Ended As Lovers' for the 1975 album *Blow By Blow*. "The Les Paul, I thought everybody's got those," said Beck, "and I wanted to speak quite clearly as me. My Les Paul sounded good, but it just sounded like … well, I won't mention who it sounded like. There wasn't much in the way of amplification variables that could make me sound like it, but as soon as I picked up this Tele, there was something there."[66]

Beck dedicated 'Cause We've Ended As Lovers' to Roy Buchanan – of whom more shortly. What the Tele master made of Beck's gesture is unknown, but in an interview the year after *Blow By Blow* came out, Buchanan had a warning for all those busily bolting 'buckers on to old Teles. "They're antiques, really, and putting a humbucker on them would be like putting a moustache on the Mona Lisa."[67]

Buchanan's note of caution was largely ignored, and for some players the Tele-plus-humbucker trend continued through the 1970s. Steve Howe, a keen guitar collector, bought a mid-'50s Tele while on tour with Yes in the States in 1974. He quickly added a neck humbucker and used it for quite a lot of that year's *Relayer* album. "The Tele was great for me then," said Howe, "and although I could make it sound like a Gibson thanks to the humbucker, the back pickup is what makes it a Telecaster."[68]

Andy Summers came to prominence with The Police later in the 1970s, though he'd had a long apprenticeship, notably with Hammond organist Zoot Money's bands. On stage with The Police, Summers almost exclusively played a Telecaster Custom, which he'd bought in California while teaching there in 1972, soon replacing the neck pickup with a humbucker. His fragmented, small-chord approach worked well on the Tele. "I've never found another guitar that sounded better," he said at the time. "It's a '61 or a '63 sunburst Custom with a Gibson humbucker in front. The back pickup has been packed underneath so it doesn't feed back at all. There's a little pre-amp built into the back of the guitar so that it will overload for a great, strong lead sound, plus an out-of-phase switch. I like simple guitars."[69]

"IT HAD THE FEEL OF A TELE AND JUST THIS BIG FAT SOUND OF THE HUMBUCKERS. IT'S A REALLY GOOD COMBINATION."
Jeff Beck on the guitar he played on 'Cause We've Ended As Lovers'

Fender reacted to the humbucker trend. The existing Telecaster Thinline model was modified in 1971 with two new Fender humbuckers. The humbucker-equipped guitar was presumably designed to send a signal that Fender was invading Gibson territory – and recognised that some players had pre-empted such a move. Fender said in a press release: "The humbucking pickups not only help eliminate feedback, they also add a gutty mid-range and bass sound." It was about as close as Fender would come to saying, "This Fender is like a Gibson."

Fender had enticed Seth Lover to California in 1967, away from the Gibson company in Michigan where Lover had famously invented Gibson's humbucking pickup in the

1950s. Warm, powerful humbuckers had given a distinctive edge to dozens of Gibson models, not least the Les Paul electrics that had come back into vogue during the late 1960s. Lover explained what his new employers were after. "The Fender sales force wanted a copy of a Gibson humbucking pickup, wanted it to sound exactly like that," he said. "The patent had not quite run out, so I designed them a pickup that looked a little different. Also, I used cunife magnets [an alloy of copper-nickel-iron], not Gibson's alnico [aluminium-nickel-cobalt]. I hesitated in making it sound exactly like the Gibson – I figured Fender was known for a brilliant type sound, so I kept a little more brilliance in the Fender pickup than there was in the Gibson."[70] Lover staggered the polepieces, with the three bass ones to the front of the cover and the three treble ones to the rear.

"A whole new spectrum of sounds"

Fender then reconsidered the way they'd blatantly replaced both pickups with humbuckers on that revised Thinline model, and came up with a more restrained arrangement for the Telecaster Custom in 1972.

This time the classic Tele lead pickup stayed put, and just the neck pickup was changed to a humbucker. Fender's marketing director Dave Gupton combined hype with prescience in his press statement about the new instrument. "Musicians looking for sound versatility will be able to do just about anything with the new Telecaster Custom," he boasted in typical ad-speak. But then he got real. "By incorporating the latest humbucking-design Fender pickup along with the unique world renowned Telecaster lead pickup, a whole new spectrum of sounds is created."

Fender were back to twin humbuckers for the Telecaster Deluxe of 1973. This seemed like a cross between the big-headstock neck of the contemporary Stratocaster (some even had Strat-style vibratos), the body of a Telecaster, and the pickups and controls of a Gibson. None of the humbucker'd Teles were very successful at the time, with potential customers generally confused, and at the time they stayed away. The humbucker-equipped Telecaster Deluxe and Custom models would both disappear from the pricelist by 1981, the Thinline two tears earlier. But as we shall see, they would become fashionable years later as some players discovered the potent combination of Tele playability and humbucker raunch.

Like many Fenders of the period, the humbucker'd Teles were fitted with a bullet truss-rod adjuster and a neck-tilt system. (The 'bullet' term described the appearance of the truss-rod adjustment nut at the headstock; the neck-tilt system was a Fender device of the time at the neck-to-body joint that allowed easier adjustment of neck pitch, or angle.) They also came with the company's new high-gloss 'thick skin' finish, achieved by spraying more than a dozen coats of polyester on to the unfortunate instrument, and today reviled by some for its plastic appearance and giveaway 1970s vibe.

Despite all this twin-coil madness, guitarists continued to be drawn to the original, unadulterated single-coil Tele, and few with more effect on their fellow musicians than the great Roy Buchanan. He had it all: a keen melodic sense coupled to economic note

Sounds of the Seventies

1972 Fender Telecaster lake placid blue

Time now to stop for a moment and enjoy a 1970s interlude as we consider some more musicians from that decade who helped to keep the Fender Telecaster on the guitarist's map. But keep in mind what the Fender factory was up to: check out the Tele (main guitar) another example of blue faded to green. Two pictures (opposite) capture Tele-toting Robbie Robertson at work with The Band: in rehearsal with Levon Helm and onstage with Rick Danko. The chap with the flowing locks (above) is Bill Harkleroad, better known to Captain Beefheart fans as Zoot Horn Rollo, his glassy Tele tone an appropriate foil for the Captain's vocalising. Bruce Springsteen hit it big in the middle of the decade with *Born To Run*, and on the jacket

here you can see him alongside his sax player Clarence Clemons brandishing his Esquire, complete with severe pickup modifications. And last but certainly not least (below) comes the great Roy Buchanan, the fabled melodic stylist who knew exactly how to get the most from his Telecaster.

choice, an astounding flair for solo dexterity, and an ability to shine with singers (including himself) or in instrumental pieces. Buchanan's main guitar was a '53 Tele which he got around 1968. "I like the old Teles because of the wood," he said, "the way the pickups are wound, the capacitors – the whole works."[71]

He set the bar in 1972 with an early single, 'Sweet Dreams', a languid, bluesy romp full of clean, instinctive Tele lines. Many fine recordings followed. Robbie Robertson of The Band said: "Roy had a command over the guitar that I couldn't comprehend. He bent the neck; he bent the strings behind the bridge. He played with both hands on the fingerboard. He used every ornament on the thing to get a noise out of it. It was like the guitar came to life. It started speaking. ... Because Roy was such a complicated person, he never played with anybody where he could be shown in his proper light. I remember hearing ... that The Rolling Stones were talking to him, wanting to try him out – and he didn't even show up."[72]

For his comeback in 1986, Buchanan evidently had a change of heart and decided to give up his beloved old Teles. "A lot of people won't want to hear this, but the new guitars are actually better than the old ones," he said, explaining that he was now using a new '86 Tele. "I mean, I would rather be driving a brand new Rolls Royce than a '55 Chevy."[73] His drink and drug battles didn't give him much longer, unfortunately, and Buchanan committed suicide in 1988, at the age of 48.

King Harvest has surely come

Robbie Robertson did some fine stuff with a Telecaster at the end of the 1960s and into the '70s on Band and Dylan/Band live dates and records. One of his peak achievements came in 'King Harvest' on The Band's 'brown' second album from 1969, where his thoughtful Tele support throughout culminates in a wonderfully dry, spiky, hesitant solo at the very close of the track. But he shines almost everywhere he plays, and it's impossible not to smile and enjoy such a masterful minimalist as he deploys harmonics, drones, volume effects and more to create a distinctive guitar voice. Much of the great work is on a Tele, but Robertson shifted to Strats in 1975.

We learned earlier about Jeff Beck's generous gift of a Telecaster to Jimmy Page. Page used that guitar in The Yardbirds and a good deal of early Led Zeppelin, on stage and in the studio. He pulled out the Tele again for one of his most revered solos, on 'Stairway To Heaven'. Page was better known by the time of its release on the untitled fourth album in 1971 for big, thick Les Paul sounds, but 'Stairway' is pure Telecaster. About six minutes into the marathon track, Page builds a careful, logical, satisfying statement on his Tele that perfectly suits the lofty surroundings.

The decade was chock full of other great Tele moments. Catfish Collins defined funk rhythm playing on James Brown's 'Sex Machine' in 1970; Bill Harkleroad aka Zoot Horn Rollo hit long, meaning notes and let them float all over Captain Beefheart's 1972 LP *Clear Spot*; Status Quo boogied endlessly on a pair of road-weary Teles, Rick Parfitt's a battered home-painted white '65 and Francis Rossi's an equally careworn '57 that went from sunburst to black to green; Sly and his brother, guitarist Freddie, sprayed Teles into the Family Stone's funky stuff; Bruce Springsteen strummed a hard-working Esquire (Telefied with a second pickup); and even Marc Bolan posed on TV with a sunburst Tele Custom as he mimed to T.Rex's 1971 Number 1 'Hot Love'.

Fender's Dave Gupton announced that 1972 had been a record year for the company, with unit production and dollar sales figures both higher than ever before. He was in little doubt that 1973 would yield still higher figures and that the trend would continue upward. A major expansion program was on at the Fullerton plant to boost output still further, completed in summer 1974 and providing the Fender operation with a new total of 289,600 square feet of production, warehouse and shipping space.

This is precisely why CBS had purchased Fender back in 1965. But the increase in the number of instruments leaving the factory inevitably affected quality. A feeling was beginning to set in that Fenders were not made like they used to be. A number of top musicians were regularly to be seen playing old guitars, now described as 'vintage' instruments, adding to the growing impression that numbers might be more important to Fender than quality. Some guitarists were becoming convinced that older instruments were somehow more playable and sounded better than new guitars.

"ROY HAD A COMMAND OVER HIS TELECASTER THAT I JUST COULDN'T COMPREHEND. THE GUITAR STARTED SPEAKING."
Robbie Robertson on Roy Buchanan

One of the earliest signs of this new old-is-best vibe came in a piece published in the *Washington Post* at the end of 1972. Reporter Tom Zito had spotted a trend that had some local musicians hunting for original Telecasters. "Available for a mere $150 in 1952," wrote Zito, more or less accurately, "this humble electric guitar has already increased in value some 500 percent. ... Proof, in the buy-it-on-time, wear-it-out and throw-it-away world of rock, that enduring value does indeed exist."

Zito contacted Leo Fender and told him that some musicians now seemed to consider a vintage Tele in a similar light to the hallowed – and immensely valuable – Stradivarius violins of 17th century Italy. Apparently the 65-year-old Fender paused, as well he might. Then he said: "Well, I'm sure a lot of musicians feel just like that about 'em. Now I'll give you an example. In 1929 I bought a Model 12 Remington. I mean, I could really hit a target with that old rifle. One time I got a jack rabbit at better than 300 yards. You see, some pieces of machinery just suit people."

The reporter then turned to Freddie Tavares at Fender, who told him that the continuing demand for Teles, old and new, was down to the sound. "Now how do you describe that? I'll tell you. It's the kind of sound that says: Listen, you bugger, I'm talkin', so shut up! It's a piercing, whining sound that forces you to pay attention, and it's filled with clear high-range harmonics. What makes it so appealing is that it makes the average ear say, 'My god, what brilliance!'"

Punkcaster rockers

The late 1970s meant punk and in the British version at least there was a fair showing for the Fender Telecaster. The most visible Tele player was Joe Strummer of The Clash (right and far right) whose stickered instrument became a punk icon right through the band's rise from London pubs to worldwide stadiums. The punk guitarist's punk guitarist was Wilko Johnson of Dr Feelgood (left), a manic onstage presence whose fluid rhythm-and-lead style drove the band with a distinctive, brittle edge. Over in California at the Fender factory, the weather was still sunny and punks rarely spotted. Just take a look at these ads from the period: there's the Telecaster as a walking vinyl record machine (left) and as a kind of techno-bird or even as lead guitar in a Three Bears jam session (right). And all the while the '70s Telecaster itself (main guitar) continued to define the current state of the Fender guitar-making style.

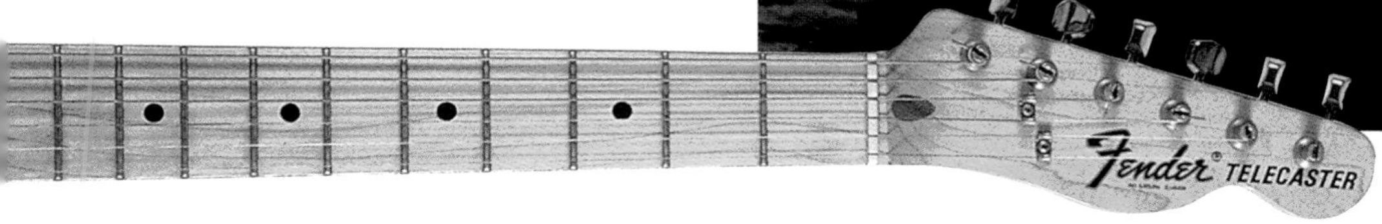

▲ **1974 Fender Telecaster**

Zito at the *Post* had the good luck to come upon guitarist Danny Gatton. Of course, we know now that he was one of the great Tele players, but back then he was just another struggling Washington guitarist, and one who sold and repaired instruments as a sideline. "The reason people want [early-'50s Telecasters] is because of that old funky Fender sound," said Gatton. "I've been getting calls for them like hotcakes. People have been paying five beans [$500] for them. … Not that I really blame them. It's all I'll play. You can do everything – squeeze all that country funk out of them. If there's a sound you can't get, don't blame it on the axe. It means you can't pick."

Tavares and Leo naturally thought that new Teles sounded as good as old ones. Gatton was equally sure that pre-1956 Teles were best. "There's all the difference in the world," he said, and continued with a list of significant changes: thicker-gauge wire in the pickup coils now that reduced fidelity; raised rather than flat pickup polepieces, producing muddier tones; less wax filling for the newer pickups, increasing feedback problems; and different value capacitors, altering the Tele's classic tone.[74]

Gatton would become a Tele player's Tele player in years to come, making influential records like *Redneck Jazz* (1978) and *88 Elmira Street* (1991) before his untimely death by his own hand in 1994. He was a constant fiddler, modifying and adapting his guitars and working closely with Joe Barden in search of the perfect pickup. A couple of Teles, a '52 and a '53, were his workhorses. "[Guitarist] Bob Berman, a good friend of Roy [Buchanan's], would come to hear me play," Gatton told an interviewer in 1983. "He'd say, 'I like what you're doing, but you've got to play an old Tele like Roy's – that's the sound!' I said that they were cheap, and pointed to the pearl on my Les Paul. Then Bob hired me on a demo session he was recording. I was about to record a solo when he handed me his '52 Tele and said, 'Play something that'll knock my socks off, and it's yours.' So I pulled out all the stops, and he gave me my first Telecaster. … Most important, the Tele gives me that dirty blues sound that I can't get from my Les Pauls."[75]

"MOST IMPORTANT, THE TELE GIVES ME THAT DIRTY BLUES SOUND THAT I CAN'T GET FROM MY LES PAULS."
Danny Gatton

The search for old guitars and the notion that they were mysteriously and inherently better grew steadily during the 1970s. Norman's Rare Guitars, established in California during the middle of the decade, was one of the newer dealers specialising in the 'vintage' requirements of rock players. Proprietor Norman Harris was in no doubt why so many guitarists were taking up older instruments – like those he offered for sale. "You simply cannot compare what I have to offer with what the big companies are mass producing today," he boasted.[76]

The first published attempt to sort out the various old Telecasters and their dates of manufacture came in Tom Wheeler's *The Guitar Book* in 1974, later more definitively in André Duchossoir's *The Fender Telecaster* (1991).

Meanwhile, over at Fender HQ in Fullerton, California, the December 1974 pricelist revealed just a few options for new Telecasters. Most of Fender's original Custom Colors had been discontinued in the late 1960s and early 1970s. By now the Telecaster was available in just six finishes: standard blond ($315), or natural (ash), sunburst, black, white, or walnut ($330 each). The regular model had the rosewood 'board of the period, but maple was an option. Left-handers and Bigsby-vibrato versions were also available (though this was the last year for now of the Bigsby option). The basic two-humbucker Tele Deluxe in walnut was $440 and the single-humbucker Custom in sunburst $345.

In Britain, punk was – depending on your viewpoint – giving a welcome opportunity to fresh young hopefuls or wiping out the idea of good musicianship. There was some good Tele action amongst it all, most visibly by Clash mainman Joe Strummer with his bashed-up black Tele covered in stickers – even though it was Mick Jones's Gibsons that provided much of the band's signature raunch. Dr Feelgood straddled the stylistic gap between pub-rock and punk, mixing old-style R&B with a thoroughly modern brutality supplied by manic Telecaster-wielding guitarist Wilko Johnson. Punks in almost everything but name and sartorial style, the Feelgoods achieved their peak of success in October 1976 when their third album, the live *Stupidity*, topped the British album charts. Johnson generally used one of his pair of '63 Teles for a brittle, seat-of-the-pants sound that harked back to the lead-and-rhythm-all-at-once style of his chief influence, Mick Green of The Pirates.

THE SEARCH FOR OLD GUITARS – NOW CALLED 'VINTAGE' – AND THE NOTION THAT THESE INSTRUMENTS WERE MYSTERIOUSLY AND INHERENTLY BETTER, GREW STEADILY DURING THE 1970s

At the Fender factory a shortlived revival began in 1977 of the Antigua finish, a light-to-dark shaded colour that had first been offered as an option during the late 1960s on some Coronado models. Back then, the finish had been adopted as an emergency measure to disguise manufacturing flaws. This time around it was deployed purely for its aesthetic appeal. Several Teles were given Antigua options, including the regular model, the Deluxe, and the Custom. This new Antigua style, now with more of a graduated tone, was matched to similarly finished pickguards. Also featured on the Antigua guitars was the new black hardware that Fender had started to use from 1975. All the plasticware – knobs, pickup covers, switch caps and all – was now black, and this certainly enhanced the overall look of the Antigua-finish instruments. It was also around this time that Fender's tuners were generally replaced by closed-cover units bought in from the German Schaller company, a supplier they used until 1983.

CBS was selling 40,000 Fender instruments a year by the end of the 1970s. A further sign of this vastly increased production was the end of the tradition for putting a date on an instrument's neck. Since the earliest days of Esquires and Broadcasters, workers had

Playing marbles with bowling balls

▸ **1984 Fender Telecaster Standard bowling ball blue**

▲ **1984 Fender Telecaster Standard bowling ball gold**

Into the 1980s, and our two representatives of Tele-playing supremacy come from each end of the spectrum. Danny Gatton (above) is a Tele player's Tele player, and the title of his 1978 album *Redneck Jazz* hinted at a couple of the constituents of his remarkable playing. Gatton would benefit from a lofty reputation among his peers as well as a Fender signature Telecaster in 1990, but four years later the troubled musician committed suicide. Andy Summers (opposite) was an experienced player when he joined The Police in the 1970s, with huge success at the end of that decade and into the 1980s. Summers used a Custom Telecaster with added neck humbucker, aiding his small-chord effects-assisted sound. In the early 1980s Fender decided to draw attention to the shortlived Telecaster Standard (the one with no through-body stringing) and produced a trial run of 50 guitars in three 'marble' or 'bowling ball' finishes, examples of which are shown on these pages. Fender decided not to pursue the idea.

▲ 1984 Fender Telecaster Standard bowling ball red

almost always pencilled and later rubber-stamped dates on the body-end of necks. It remains about the most reliable way to date a Fender of the period – leaving aside the question of fakes. But from 1973 to the early 1980s Fender stopped doing it. Presumably they were simply too busy.

By 1976 Fender had a five-acre facility under one roof in Fullerton and employed over 750 workers. John Page, who would run Fender's Custom Shop from the late 1980s until the early 2000s, started working for Fender in 1978, spending some months on the production line before moving to R&D. He said there was rampant departmentalism at Fender in the late 1970s. "You couldn't even tell Purchasing what part you wanted or where you wanted it from, all you could tell them was the spec of the part you wanted," Page explained. "It was so compartmentalised, and virtually no one got to know anyone else in any of the other departments. There was no communication."

Page also recalled his horror when he discovered one of the CBS executives of the time cheerfully disposing of Fender's history. "This guy came through our office and he was putting green dots on all our guitars," said Page. "I asked what he was doing. 'Oh well, I got this great programme, I'm gonna give these away to dealers, yes sir.' What! And before we were able to stop it, he had given away about 80 percent of our original prototypes and samples."[77]

By 1979 the Fender pricelist showed ten electric models in the line with a basic Tele at $535 (rosewood neck) or $580 (maple), a single-humbucker Custom at $580 (rosewood) or $615 (maple), and a two-humbucker Deluxe at $685 (maple only). The Telecasters sat among seven other electrics (Bronco, Jazzmaster, Lead, Musicmaster, Mustang, Starcaster, and Stratocaster).

Colour schemes were brightened during the 1980s, with the shortlived International Colors in 1981 and then the Custom Colors and Stratobursts of '82. Some of the new hues were distinctly lurid, such as Capri Orange, Aztec Gold, or Bronze Stratoburst, and they were not much liked at the time. In 1983 there was a short run of marble 'bowling ball' finishes, in red, blue or yellow. But at least the idea of a decent selection of Custom Colors seemed to be back in place.

With generally trimmed model lines and a massive output from the factories, it was hard to resist the feeling as the 1980s dawned that the newly-important calculations of the balance sheet had become firmly established at Fender and taken precedence over the company's former creativity. At the start of the decade, CBS management decided that they needed some new blood to help reverse a decline in Fender's fortunes. Income had been climbing spectacularly to 1980 – it had tripled in that year from 1971's $20 million – but re-investment in the company was wavering.

So during 1981 key personnel were recruited from the American musical instrument division of Yamaha, the giant Japanese company. John McLaren was hired as head of CBS Musical Instruments overall, and among the other newcomers from Yamaha were Bill Schultz and Dan Smith. Schultz was hired as Fender president and Smith as director of marketing electric guitars. Smith recalled: "We were brought in to turn the reputation of

Fender around and to get it so it was making money again. It was starting to lose money, and at that point in time everybody hated Fender. We thought we knew how bad it was. We took it for granted that they could make Stratocasters and Telecasters the way they used to make them. But it turned out we were wrong. So many things had been changed in the plant."[78]

Schultz was given the go-ahead by CBS to try to improve matters. Among the first changes Smith made on his arrival was to revise the look of the Telecaster. "One of the things that had happened in the '70s was that CBS had brought in a CNC [computer controlled] machine and modified the shape of the Telecaster so it would work with that machine," Smith explained. "So if you look at Teles from the '70s to about 1982 or so, when we got it back to where it should be, the shoulder on the left-hand side is weird. It was too low, and that little cut-out that happens right at the neck had a larger radius. They had lost the curve that goes from the left side shoulder down into the cutaway on the right side. We said hey, you can't change that shape! We fixed it so your eye picks up a nice smooth transition, a nice French curve from one side to the next."[79]

A Fender Telecaster made in Japan

Schultz recommended a large investment package, primarily aimed at modernising the factory. This had the immediate effect of virtually stopping production while new machinery was brought in and staff were re-trained. Another recommendation that Schultz had been working on was to start alternative production of Fenders in Japan. The reason was relatively straightforward: Fender's sales were being hammered by the onslaught of copies produced in the orient. These Japanese copyists made their biggest profits in their own domestic market, so the best place to hit back at them was in Japan – by making and selling guitars there.

When the Japanese had started emulating classic American guitars in the early 1970s, most Western makers didn't see much to worry about. Later, the quality of the Japanese instruments improved, but some American makers still kept their heads stuck firmly in the sand. Dave Gupton, vice president of Fender by 1978, said: "Fender is not adversely affected by the Japanese copies as perhaps some of the other major manufacturers, because we have been able to keep our costs pretty much in line."[80]

That casual attitude changed dramatically in a few short years. By the start of the 1980s the U.S. dollar had soared in value relative to the Japanese yen. Coupled with the high quality of many Japanese guitars, this meant that instruments built in the orient were making a real impact on the international guitar market. Many emulated Fender and Gibson models. "We had to stop this plethora of copies," said Smith. "A lot of these companies basically told Bill Schultz and me that they were going to bury us. They were ripping us off, and what we really needed to do was to get these guys where it hurt – back in their own marketplace."[81]

With the blessing of CBS, negotiations began with two Japanese distributors, Kanda Shokai and Yamano Music, to establish the Fender Japan company. The joint venture was

Yesterday once more

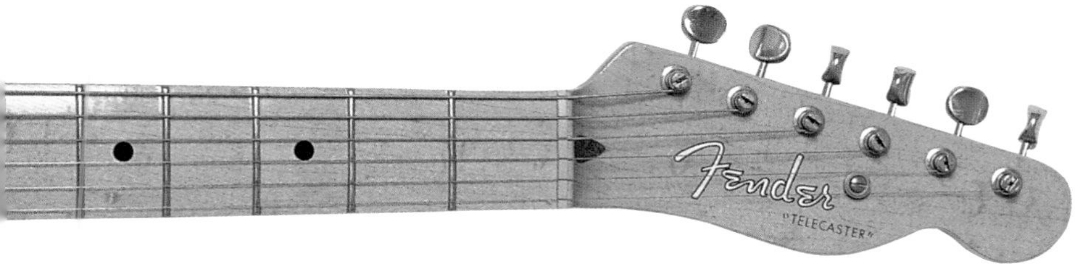

▲ **1984 Fender '52 Telecaster**

Old Fender hand Freddie Tavares began work on Fender's first modern reissue in 1980. So-called 'vintage' instruments had grown in stature during the 1970s and prices moved up for good, playable, original guitars, especially early Fenders and Gibsons. The result of Tavares's industry was the '52 Telecaster (main guitar). It was publicised in Fender's 1982 catalogue (opposite, top right) even though the US-made examples did not come on stream until the following year. Fender began Japanese production at this time, and some of the earliest models from that source were branded Squier (ad, above). The name came from a string company that Fender had acquired some years earlier (60s ad, opposite). Meanwhile, one of the few jazz guitarists attracted to the Tele was Mike Stern (above, left) who played with Miles Davis in the early 1980s and released his first solo ablum, *Neesh*, in 1983.

officially established in March 1982 combining the forces of Fender, Kanda and Yamano. Fender U.S. licensed Fender Japan the right to have Fender guitars built within Japan for the Japanese market. After discussions with Tokai, Kawai, and others, the factory finally chosen to build guitars for Fender Japan was Fujigen, based in Matsumoto, some 130 miles north-west of Tokyo. Fujigen was best known in the West for the excellence of its Ibanez-brand instruments. Fujigen had been making Greco copies of Fender and Kanda Shokai had been selling them, so they were well prepared to make and sell Fender guitars.

Meanwhile in the States the new management team were working on a strategy to return Fender to its former glory. The plan was, quite simply, for Fender to copy itself, by recreating the guitars that, as we've seen, many players and collectors were spending large sums of money to acquire: the 'vintage' Fender guitars made back in the company's glory years in the 1950s and 1960s. Freddie Tavares, still a consultant to Fender R&D, began work around 1980 on a Vintage Telecaster, planned as a re-creation of a 1952 model. It was to be the first modern reissue of a vintage-style Fender guitar.

IN THE EARLY 1980s, FENDER BOUGHT SOME VINTAGE FENDER GUITARS. "THAT'S RIGHT," SAID DAN SMITH, "WE WENT OUT AND BOUGHT BACK OUR OWN PRODUCT!"

At the July NAMM trade show in 1981 Fender showed a prototype. Dan Smith arrived at the company a month later. "This supposed '52 Telecaster had polyester finish, the wrong body shape, a whole bunch of stuff wrong with it," said Smith. "I told them we can't ship that. So we shut down the vintage reissue series. We brought in Ted Greene, a great guitar player here in Southern California, who had I think 13 or 14 old Broadcasters and Nocasters and Telecasters. We spent a lot of time with him and his Teles, talking through things and making sure we had all the details right."[82]

The team searched further to assist in their proposed re-creations of vintage instruments. R&D man John Page travelled with Smith to vintage guitar dealer Ax In Hand in Illinois where they took more measurements and photographs and paint-tests from relevant old Fenders. They also bought some vintage Fender instruments. "That's right," laughed Smith, "we went out and bought back our own product!"[83]

Such industry resulted in Fender's first Vintage reissue series, which began to appear in 1982. The guitars consisted of the revised '52 Telecaster, plus a maple-neck '57 and rosewood-board '62 Strat. Production of the Vintage reissues was planned to start in 1982 at Fender U.S. (Fullerton) and at Fender Japan (Fujigen), but the changes underway at the American factory meant that the U.S. versions did not come on-stream until early 1983, and the factory there was not up to full speed until the start of '84.

The July 1983 pricelist pitched the '52 Telecaster reissue at $895, which was $445 more than the regular Tele. That same month, Guitar Trader, a dealer based in New Jersey and specialising in vintage instruments, offered a 1954 Telecaster for sale at $3,000. It was the most expensive guitar in their inventory except for a handful of 1950s Les Paul Standards and a Flying V. Their Tele was blond with maple neck, black pickguard and level-polepiece lead pickup and, said Guitar Trader, it was "fully intact and supplied with original formfit hardcase" and was "the most sought-after style of Telecaster produced".[84]

Fender's Vintage Tele reproduction was not exact enough for some die-hard collectors, but the idea seemed sound enough. If there was a market for old guitars, then why not for guitars that looked like the old ones? Guitarists knew that the instruments had to feel and play right, too, however – the very attributes that made the older Teles so appealing. Clearly, Fender had more work to do. But they were definitely onto something.

Dan Smith and his colleagues at Fender U.S. received samples of the Japanese-made Vintage reissues before U.S. production started, and he remembered their reaction to the high quality of these oriental Fender re-creations. "Everybody came up to inspect them and the guys almost cried, because the Japanese product was so good. It was what we were having a hell of a time trying to do."[85]

Fender Japan's guitars at this stage were being made only for the internal Japanese market, but Fender's European agents were putting pressure on the Fullerton management for a budget-price Fender to compete with the multitude of exported models being sold in Europe and elsewhere by other Japanese manufacturers.

So Fender Japan made some less costly versions of the Vintage Tele and Strat reissues for European distribution in 1982. These were distinguished at first by the addition of a small 'Squier Series' logo on the tip of the headstock. This was soon changed, with a large 'Squier' replacing the Fender logo. Thus the Squier brand was born. The name came from a string-making company, V.C. Squier of Michigan, that Fender had acquired in the mid 1960s. Victor Carroll Squier was born in 19th-century Boston, the son of an English immigrant, and became a violin maker, moving to Battle Creek, Michigan, where he founded his string-making firm in 1890. The company operated at the same Battle Creek building from 1927 to 1972, when CBS relocated the operation within the town.

FENDER'S FIRST VINTAGE REISSUES BEGAN TO APPEAR IN 1982. IF THERE WAS A MARKET FOR OLD GUITARS, THEN WHY NOT FOR GUITARS THAT LOOKED LIKE THE OLD ONES?

Meanwhile, toward the end of 1983, with the U.S. Fender factory still not up to the scale of production the team wanted, Schultz and Smith decided to have Fender Japan build a couple of instruments for the U.S. market. They approved Japanese production of a Squier-brand '70s-style Telecaster and Strat. These, together with the earlier Squier Vintage Teles and Strats, saw the start of the sale of Fender Japan products around the world, and the move by Fender to become an international manufacturer of guitars.

"It taught us, contrary to what the guys believed at Fender six or seven years before, that people would buy Fender guitars with 'made in Japan' on them," Smith said. "In fact

Getting close to that elite country boy

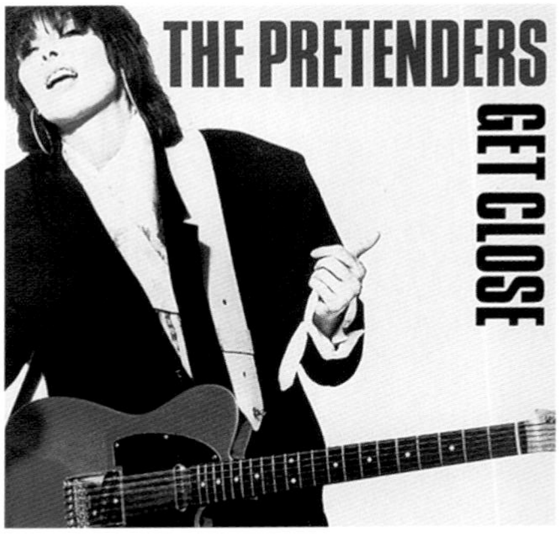

▼ 1983 Fender Gold Elite Telecaster ruby red

▲ **1983 Fender Gold Elite Telecaster emerald green**

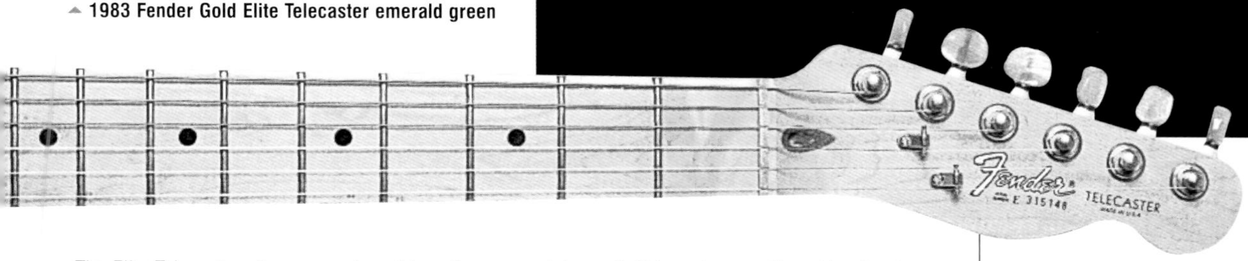

The Elite Telecasters (two examples pictured) were a radical departure from traditional design, intended to stake out new ground for the modern instrument in contrast to the successful vintage-style reissues. But the Elites, launched in 1983, did not last for much more than a year on the Fender pricelist, even in the upscale gold-hardware variant shown here (the Gold Elite above has the optional stick-on pickguard). Telecasters continued to attract high-profile pop players: Chrissie Hynde of The Pretenders (above) featured her favourite blue Tele on the jacket of their 1986 album *Get Close*. Albert Lee (opposite) was a confirmed Tele fan for much of his career and played one on many of his recordings, including the influential electric-and-acoustic 'Country Boy'.

I really believe that our introduction of those instruments, worldwide and in the U.S.A., was what legitimised buying Japanese guitars."[86] Certainly there had been a resistance by many musicians to the cheap image associated with Japanese-made guitars, but the rise in quality of instruments from brands such as Ibanez, Yamaha, Fernandes, Aria, Tokai – and Fender and Squier – wiped away a good deal of this prejudice and gave oriental guitars a new popularity and respectability.

At the U.S. factory in 1983 some cost-cutting changes were made to the Standard Telecaster and Stratocaster. These were the result of the dollar's strength and the consequent difficulty in selling U.S.-made products overseas, where they were becoming increasingly high-priced. Savings had to be made, so the Tele was deprived of its tone-enhancing through-body stringing – just as Fender had done briefly back in the late 1950s. It was still an ill-conceived change, and many onlookers who had applauded the improvements made since '81 groaned inwardly at the familiar signs of economics apparently taking precedence once again over playability and sound. Fortunately, this mutant variety of a key Fender model lasted only until the end of 1984, by which time its list price was $589.

Another shortlived guitar from the same period was the Elite Telecaster (and accompanying Stratocaster), intended as a radical new high-end version of the old faithful. The Elite sold for $895 and had two new-design pickups designed for humbucking noise cancellation and single-coil brilliance and linked to 'active' circuitry. This was a popular kind of system at the time, and a first for Fender. It incorporated a battery-powered pre-amp to boost the signal and widen the tonal range – and only a few of these new sounds would be familiar to traditional Tele players. The bridge/tailpiece was also restyled to incorporate six individual saddles. There were good points – the new pickups, the effective active circuitry, and an improved truss-rod design – but they tended to be overlooked. The Elite Tele and Strat (which was saddled with the poor new Freeflyte vibrato system) were dropped by the end of '84.

"MY STYLE EVOLVED AROUND THAT GUITAR. YOU DEVELOP A STYLE ON A TELECASTER THAT YOU DON'T DEVELOP ON ANOTHER GUITAR."
Albert Lee

Perhaps the look of the Elite Tele was in reaction to Schecter and in particular to Pete Townshend's use of a Tele-style guitar made from Schecter parts. Schecter was a U.S. firm among the leaders of a new fad for replacement parts to soup up existing guitars; not just pickups, but brass hardware or fancy pickguards and knobs, in fact anything to give a dusty guitar a fresh look or sound. Fender had already reacted to the craze with its own lines of brass hardware, Standard Brass and Brassmaster, launched in 1980, claiming like the rest that brass aided sustain and improved overall tone. Fender's business and production headaches didn't help them in the 1980s, and new competing styles of solidbody electric guitars were appearing, notably the 'superstrat' style popularised by Jackson and Charvel. But the Telecaster could still be seen and heard in some engaging company.

Fender's image could not have suffered too much when Freddie Mercury picked up a white Tele to strum as Queen began their performance of 'Crazy Little Thing Called Love' at 1985's Live Aid, the famine-relief benefit that grabbed a remarkable global audience of 1.4 billion people in over 150 countries.

Chrissie Hynde was often seen with a striking blue Tele at Pretenders gigs, but guitarist James Honeyman-Scott grabbed it in the studio for his gorgeously crafted solo on 'Kid' for the band's first album, released in 1980. At the other end of the musical spectrum sat two great Tele men: supreme country Tele picker Ray Flacke, heard for example on the Ricky Scaggs albums *Waiting For The Sun to Shine* (1982) and *Highways And Heartaches* (1983), and Mike Stern, whose keen work on the '82 live Miles Davis album *We Want Miles* marked a relatively rare example of a Tele in jazz.

Albert Lee was a confirmed Tele fan who'd played with Sonny Curtis's Crickets and Emmylou Harris – and at one point had the unlikely job of guitarist with Eric Clapton. His solo albums too pricked the ears of plenty of other guitarists, the 1986 instrumental album *Speechless* being a particularly good example. But it's the 1979 track 'Country Boy' that has come for many to define his deft picking, full of tumbling arpeggios from his steely Tele (as well as some fierce flat-top work).

In a 1981 interview Lee said he'd played a Tele since 1963. The first one had been a rosewood-board model, probably a '59 or a '60. "It was pretty beaten up," he recalled. "The guy at the store said, 'Look, a James Burton guitar.' It seemed really Mickey Mouse compared to [my previous guitar, a] Les Paul Custom, but as soon as I played it I thought: This is great. It sounded so live, so electric – more so than anything I'd ever played. From then on it was always number one. My style evolved around that guitar. ... You develop a style on a Tele that you don't develop on another guitar. I suppose my favourite now is my '53 Tele."[87]

String-bending with The Hellecasters

Jerry Donahue was another Tele man who'd played widely with others – as a member of Fotheringay and Fairport Convention, and with Joan Armatrading, Gerry Rafferty, Chris Rea and many others in the studio and on the road – and in 1986 released a firm solo statement of his guitar preference, the *Telecasting* album. When someone like Danny Gatton called him "the string-bending king of the planet" any players who hadn't already twigged Donahue's importance were sure to take notice. Later, in the early 1990s, he would become a founder member of an astonishing Tele trio, the Hellecasters, along with Will Ray and John Jorgensen. At the time of writing, Donahue was playing his Tele-style signature Peavey Omniac with a revived Yardbirds.

"First thing I did with my Tele back in the late '60s when I moved to one after using Strats was to get rid of the neck pickup," said Donahue. "I never thought it was balanced with the bridge pickup. It's great if you want to play country and then you want to play jazz.

Casting around for a new standard

Fender's new American Standard guitars redefined the modern look of the regular models following the management buy-out of the company in 1985. The revised Tele (main guitar) appeared in 1988 with 22 big frets, a fatter-sounding bridge pickup, and a six-saddle bridge, all designed to appeal to current players. It worked: with little tweaks along the way the model is still in production today, known since 2001 as the American Telecaster. Tele supremo Jerry Donahue (opposite) made a statement of intent on his 1986 *Telecasting* album (right), and Fender made Donahue signature models (prototype, opposite) from 1992 to 2001. A Japanese-made attempt to embrace fashionable Superstrat-style features resulted in the shortlived Contemporary Telecaster (opposite, below).

▲ 1990 Fender Jerry Donahue Telecaster prototype

▼ 1991 Fender American Standard Telecaster

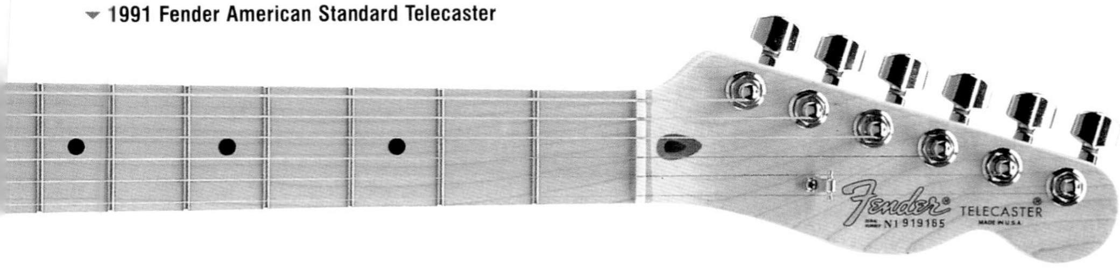

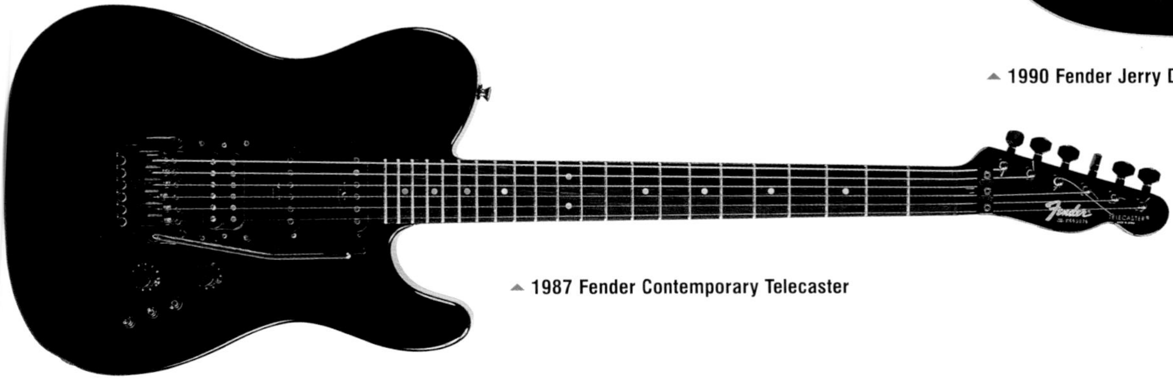

▲ 1987 Fender Contemporary Telecaster

That was probably Leo's goal, for people who wanted to play what he would have considered 'both styles'.

"I put a Strat pickup in the neck position because that was the sound I probably liked most from the Strat," Donahue continued, "besides the in-between sound that I'd found by accident along with a host of others on the three-way switch. I never fell out of love with the Strat, but the Tele just gradually became my main instrument over the years. With Fairport and Joan Armatrading I'd be swapping back and forth, but when I put out that album called *Telecasting*, the Tele became *the* guitar for me."[88]

IN 1985 CBS SOLD FENDER TO "AN INVESTOR GROUP LED BY WILLIAM SCHULTZ, PRESIDENT OF FENDER MUSICAL INSTRUMENTS"

For a variety of reasons, CBS decided during 1984 that they had finally had enough of the music business and wanted to sell Fender Musical Instruments. A newspaper report in January 1985 detailed the reasons. Essentially, CBS blamed Japanese competition for Fender's recent losses. "The Fullerton-based firm's last domestic guitar manufacturing unit, which employs 60 senior craftsmen who build top-of-the-line instruments for professional musicians, is scheduled to be shut down February 1st," added the reporter.

"Company officials say tentative plans call for the continued manufacture of electric pianos until the end of February at the plant in this Orange County community 25 miles southeast of Los Angeles. The future of the company's famed product lines – the guitars pioneered by Leo Fender, pianos by Harold Rhodes, Rogers drums, and Squier guitar strings – will depend on Fender's new owner, who must decide which ones to continue and which, if any, will be made in the United States."

The report went on to explain that the Fender name and business were being sold separately from the 250,000-plus-square-foot manufacturing plant. "There are a lot of broken hearts around Fullerton," said former CBS musical instruments division president John McLaren. The newspaper pointed out that McLaren, Schultz and their team had tried to turn the company around between 1981 and 1983. McLaren had left Fender a year ago. One estimate put sales of Fender guitars down 50 percent in the last three years. "CBS does not report financial statistics for its division separately," said the newspaper, "but attributed an $8.3 million Columbia Group operating loss for the third quarter of 1984 in part to 'continued losses in the musical instruments business'."

The news report speculated that the U.S. guitar industry's problems were not due solely to the Japanese. It suggested that the baby boom generation was past the prime instrument-buying age and, in a still familiar phrase, that "today's young people seem to be more interested in video games and computers than guitars". The newspaper also reckoned that some fault lay with the corporate giants who began snapping up the best instrument manufacturers during the 1960s but were "ill-suited to running businesses in which success depended so much on craftsmanship and personal service".[89]

CBS invited offers for Fender, and by the end of January 1985, almost exactly 20 years since they had acquired it, CBS confirmed that they would sell Fender to "an investor group led by William Schultz, president of Fender Musical Instruments". The contract was formalised in February and the sale completed in March for $12.5 million. It's impossible not to immediately compare this figure with the $13 million that CBS originally paid for the company back in 1965.

With the hectic months of negotiations and financing behind them, Schultz and his team could now run Fender for themselves (and a number of investment banks, of course). The problems they faced were legion, but probably the most pressing was the fact that the Fullerton buildings were not included in the deal.

The machine stops

So U.S. production of Fenders stopped in February 1985 – although the new team had been stockpiling bodies and necks, and had acquired some existing inventory of completed guitars as well as production machinery. The company went from employing over 800 people in early 1984 down to just over 100 in early 1985. "Scary but exciting" is how Dan Smith described it at the time. "We're not going to be in the position to be able to make any mistakes," he continued. "There'll be nobody behind us with a big cheque-book if we have a bad month."[90]

Administration headquarters were established in Brea, California, not far from Fullerton. Six years later Fender would move admin from Brea to Scottsdale, Arizona, where it remains today. A new factory also had to be found, of course, and Fender searched for a site in the general Orange County area of Los Angeles.

The Japanese operation became Fender's lifeline, providing much-needed product to a company with had no U.S. factory. All the guitars in Fender's 1985 catalogue were made in Japan, including the new Contemporary Telecasters and Strats, the first Fenders with the increasingly fashionable heavy-duty vibrato units and string-clamps. These seemed particularly odd on a Telecaster. Production in Japan was based on a handshake agreement that Fujigen would continue to supply Fender with guitars after CBS left the picture. One estimate put as much as 80 percent of the guitars that Fender U.S. sold from around the end of 1984 to the middle of 1986 as made in Japan.

In the midst of this activity, the dollar had started to weaken against other currencies, and Fender again had trouble competing on price. So they looked to another of their offshore acoustic guitar producers, the Young Chang Akki Co of Seoul, South Korea, to make electric guitars. Smith remembered Fender's first truly Korean guitars were pretty good: these were the Squier Standard Teles and Strats that began to appear in 1985 and lasted around three years. A number of Squier models are still made in Korean factories today (and some Fender-brand guitars too), while the lowest-price Squiers are usually made in China or Indonesia.

Back in the United States, Fender had finally established their new factory at Corona, about 20 miles east of the now defunct Fullerton site. Production started on a very limited

Strange customs and signed headstocks

◂ **1994 Fender Egyptian Telecaster**

▲ **1990 Fender James Burton Telecaster black/gold**

▼ **1989 Fender Telecaster 40th Anniversary**

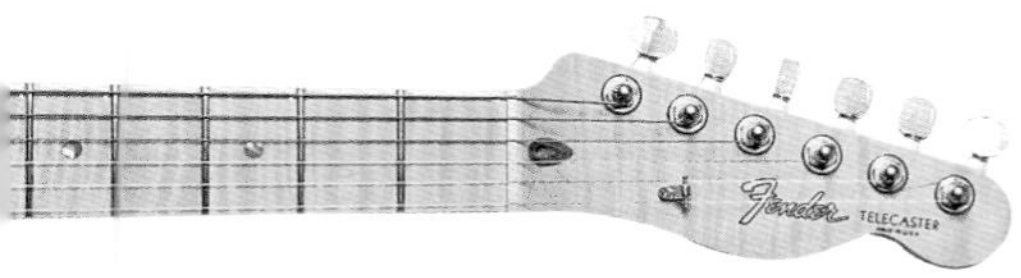

Fender's Custom Shop was officially established at the Corona factory in California at the start of 1987. The intention at first was to make one-off guitars for individual customers. Shop founders John Page (above, left) and Michael Stevens (right) are pictured early in 1987 working on their first commission, a foam green left-handed Thinline Telecaster for Elliot Easton of The Cars. Since then the Shop has developed to its present three-way role. First are the continuing one-offs, such as this Egyptian Tele (opposite) by Master Builder Fred Stuart. Second are limited editions, like the 40th Anniversary Telecaster (left, below) produced in an edition of 300 instruments. The third type of Custom Shop guitar comes as a line of catalogued models, including the 'period detail' Time Machine instruments (see page 110-111) and some signature guitars. The first Fender signature guitar in production was the Eric Clapton Strat of 1988, but discussions had begun earlier with Tele king James Burton, who waited until 1990 for his first Fender signature model to appear (pictured left).

scale toward the end of 1985 when they were building only about five guitars per day for the Vintage reissue series. But Smith and his colleagues wanted to re-establish the U.S. side of Fender's production with a good, basic Telecaster (and of course a Stratocaster, Precision Bass, and Jazz Bass). The attraction was that these guitars would involve very little new costs and would, the company hoped, be seen as a continuation of the very best of Fender's long-standing American traditions. That plan translated into the American Standard models. For this series the Telecaster was updated with a 22-fret neck and a six-saddle bridge and was launched (along with the two basses) in 1988 at $599.99, two years after the corresponding Strat.

The team had learned from recent work that the focus of the new American Standard had to be on the Tele's great strength: simplicity. Smith said they had effectively started the idea with the first Standard models at the start of the '80s. "We wanted to make a good quality, standard instrument that better addressed modern playing styles, and at a reasonable price. As George Blanda and I worked on the American Standard Strat and that bridge design, we knew the bridge saddles would work nicely for the Telecaster. So George designed a bridge plate. We gave the guitar a bigger fingerboard radius that we figured could help get an action that appealed more to Gibson guys but didn't feel much different to Fender guys, and we made the neck a little wider to accommodate modern styles, with bigger frets."

All that was pretty obvious, said Smith. But a major change was to redesign the bridge pickup. "We found that by eliminating the plate on the bottom of the pickup and moving to a brass bridge plate, in combination with the saddles, it made for a fatter sounding bridge pickup, which is what a lot of guys were looking for. It still had a nice twank or whatever you want to call it, a nice spiky, bitey sound, but it was fatter sounding and sounded better through distortion."[91] As we'll see, the American Standard turned into the American Series in 2000.

Were you looking for something a little different, sir?

In the mid 1980s the Fender Custom Shop was officially established at the Corona plant. It began so that Fender could build one-offs and special orders for players who had the money and the inclination. While this role remains – customers have included everyone from Bob Dylan and Pops Staples to David Bowie and Kurt Cobain – the Shop today has a wider part to play in Fender's expanding business.

Michael Stevens and John Page officially started the Custom Shop in January 1987. Their very first official job was to make a left-handed Telecaster Thinline in Foam Green for Elliot Easton of The Cars. The order was placed at the end of February 1987, and John Page completed the instrument on August 10th.

Today, the Custom Shop's activities effectively divide into three. First there are the one-offs, or 'Master Built' guitars as the Custom Shop calls them, and these are exactly what most people would understand as the work of a custom shop: instruments made by one person – one of the Shop's Master Builders – with acute attention to detail and a price to match. Truly bizarre instruments tend to come in a further sub-division of the one-offs known as 'art guitars'. Master Builder Fred Stuart's Egyptian Telecaster, made in 1994, was the first Fender art guitar. It had pyramids, snakes, and runes hand-carved by George Amicay into a finish of Corian synthetic stone. Another was Master Builder Chris Fleming's 2004 Leather Hula Esquire, covered in hand-tooled leather by Nevena Christi and intended to convey something of a surfing Hawaiian vibe.

"These special art guitars take a long time to build and are very, very expensive," explained John Page. "We turned down $75,000 for an Aztec Telecaster and $50,000 for a Bird-o'-Fire Strat. These guitars are done not so much as a response to a customer's request, but more because the builder has an idea and goes ahead and makes it."[92]

The second type of Custom Shop product today is the limited edition, a special numbered run of anything from a handful to hundreds of a specific model. The 40th Anniversary Telecaster of 1988 was the Shop's first limited-edition production run. (At that time, most people including Fender themselves believed that the first Broadcaster/Telecaster had been produced in 1948, which explained the out-by-two-years timing.)

Third, the Custom Shop now makes a set line of catalogued models, which began in 1992. There are 'team built' models made by Team Builders as well as 'team built custom' guitars, essentially more customised versions of the former. By 2005 the Shop's catalogued Telecasters consisted of five Custom Artist models, the various Time Machine guitars, a couple of Flat Head models with twin humbuckers, and a Custom Classic, the Custom Shop version of the American Series.

The first signature guitar produced by Fender was the Eric Clapton Stratocaster, which went on sale to the public in 1988, but the first musician with whom Fender informally discussed the possibility of a signature model was Telecaster king James Burton. "I figured that Leo Fender had already made two of the finest guitars," recalled Burton. "What do you do to improve those or make them different? And I thought well, factory-wise, Fender haven't put together a three-pickup Tele. So my idea was to make a three-pickup Tele and to experiment with the pickups I liked. My first intention was to do the pink paisley Tele as my signature model, but Fender made an agreement with the Japanese to take over the copy of the pink paisley. My guitar would be made in the States."[93]

"I FIGURED LEO FENDER HAD ALREADY MADE TWO OF THE FINEST GUITARS, AND I THOUGHT WELL, FENDER HAVEN'T PUT TOGETHER A THREE-PICKUP TELECASTER."
James Burton on his signature Tele

Burton had to wait until 1990 for his signature Telecaster to appear. It had three single-coil pickups in a Strat layout, and some were finished in a paisley pattern much more lurid than his original Red Paisley model. A number of Fender signature models have followed

Scruggs, set necks, and classics

The 1990s saw Fender attempting to diversify the Telecaster line while still recognising that a regular trad-style model held sway with many guitarists. Frank Black (right) of The Pixies was one of those enthusiastic Tele players. Signature models continued to bolster the Fender catalogue, including a tribute to Byrds man Clarence White (main guitar) who had died at the age of just 29 back in 1973. It duplicated White's favoured neck pickup, Scruggs tuners, and the on-board B-bender string-pull device that he'd invented with Byrds drummer Gene Parsons. The Custom Shop's American Classic (oppsite, centre) was an unusual three-pickup upscale take on the American Standard, while the Set Neck models (Country Artist, opposite, left) allowed Fender a rare move away from their customary bolt-on neck joint, into Gibson territory. The vintage look did survive: on the Japanese 50s Telecaster (opposite, right) and the continuing US '52 Telecaster (catalogue, opposite, below).

▲ **1993 Fender Clarence White Telecaster**

◀ 1992 Fender Set Neck Telecaster Country Artist

▶ 1995 Fender American Classic Telecaster

▶ 1997 Fender 50s Telecaster

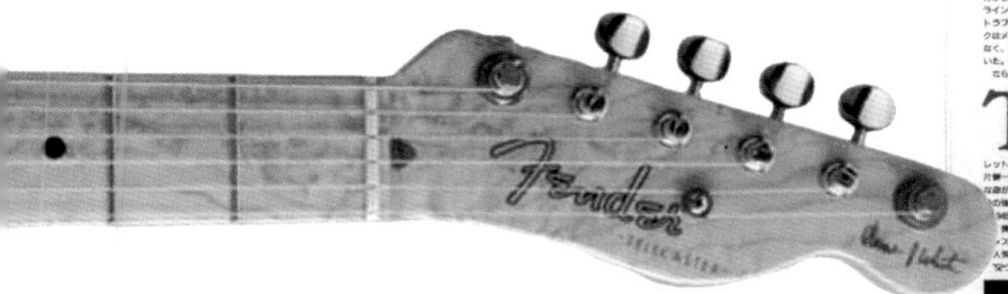

– some made in the Custom Shop, others from Corona or further afield – and each one is generally endowed with features favoured by the named artist. At various times there have been signature Telecaster models named for Jimmy Bryant, Albert Collins, Jerry Donahue, Nokie Edwards, Danny Gatton, Merle Haggard, Waylon Jennings, John 5, John Jorgensen, Buck Owens, Rick Parfitt, Will Ray, Francis Rossi, Muddy Waters, and Clarence White.

Recently there was a Seymour Duncan Esquire, modelled on the guitar that Jeff Beck swapped with pickup-man Duncan back in the 1970s. Beck was of course sent one of the new 2003 models. "I opened the box and I thought: they're having a laugh, they've sent my guitar back," he recalled. "It had every dig, every scratch, every little bit of ink stain. I'd written something on it and it sank into the wood: they've done that. Quite amusing. So I've got the repro and someone else has got the real thing. They've even got it accurate to the point where the treble control doesn't work, because it didn't work on mine. Either that," laughed Beck, "or they didn't hook it up."[94]

The Tele Plus of 1990 offered a wider choice of pickup tones by combining three of Fender's low-noise/no-string-pull Lace Sensor single-coil units, with two grouped at the bridge that could be switched in together as a humbucker. A shortlived later version opted for the Burton-type layout with three single-coils arranged Strat-style. Three-pickup Telecasters in the Fender line at the time of writing are the various made-in-Mexico Nashville Teles, introduced in 1999, and the U.S. James Burton signature model.

"I TELL PEOPLE I'VE HAD MY TELECASTER SO LONG WE HAD TO CONVERT IT FROM COAL POWER TO ELECTRICITY."
Bill Kirchen

Aside from the shortlived Esprit and Flame guitars of 1984 – and the Esprit was revived for 2005's Squier Master Series – Fender has not strayed much from its customary bolt-on-neck construction. However, three new Set Neck Teles in 1991 offered the glued joint, enabling the fashionable smooth, heel-less junction where neck meets body. Some players find this more comfortable and usefully playable. "We always try to have something in our line to interest someone who likes Gibson," said Dan Smith.[95]

Following the success of the Vintage reissue series, introduced in 1982, Fender Japan marketed more models that re-created many of the guitars from Fender's past, including reproductions of the Paisley, Blue Flower, Rosewood, and Thinline Telecasters. In 1992 Fender U.S. came up with the term 'Collectables' to cover a selection of these Japanese instruments sold in the U.S.A., including various vintage-style Teles and Strats. More recently the names have changed again, with reissues organised into the Classic Series from Mexico, the American Vintage guitars from the U.S. Corona factory, and the Time Machine models from the Custom Shop.

A new Fender factory was established in Ensenada, Mexico, in 1987, 180 miles south of Los Angeles, just across the California/Mexico border. (Non-American readers may be confused by references to Fender's 'Baja California' factory. This is the Mexican plant: Ensenada is in an area of Mexico sometimes known as Baja California.) The first Mexican Fender guitars began to appear in 1991, including the Standard Telecaster plus a Strat, P-Bass, and Jazz Bass.

There was no shortage of Tele players during the 1990s. Blur's fine *Parklife* album appeared in 1994 with Graham Coxon often opting for a Tele, and by the end of the decade his main recording and live guitars were two U.S. reissue '52 Telecasters, with new pickups added for what he called "a more modern voicing".[96] Frank Black of The Pixies and Chuck Prophet of Green On Red often selected a Tele, and Beck – that's Beck Hansen; Jeff Beck was well into Strats by now – was regularly seen live with a stock new Tele, sometimes with a friendly unicorn decoration on the body. Jeff Buckley appeared solo with little more than his Tele in support on *Live At Sin-E*, his pre-fame 1993 EP.

Bill Kirchen was with Commander Cody & The Lost Planet Airmen in the 1970s and played the fine Telecaster lead on the group's only hit single, 'Hot Rod Lincoln', in 1972. By the 1990s he was out on his own, and included a remarkable remake of that song on his *Hot Rod Lincoln Live!* CD in 1997, with Kirchen impersonating everyone from Buck Owens to The Sex Pistols in a brilliantly conceived guitar interlude. "You can hear the same Telecaster recorded in 1971 with its original pickups on the Commander Cody version, and then again on the same song more than a quarter of a century later," said Kirchen, marvelling at the longevity of his enduring Fender.

He got his Tele upon moving to San Francisco in the late 1960s. "Pete Townshend had just come through and busted his SG, and this guy sitting next to me at the gig wanted an SG and I wanted a Telecaster. I wanted to be like Don Rich and he wanted to be like Pete Townshend – so we traded. Bingo! And I still use that Tele today. My nickname for it is the coal-burner, because I tell people I've had it so long we had to convert it from coal power to electricity. Young kids are not exactly sure of their timelines and scratch their heads and think about that. If you tell them that when you first got this guitar pterodactyls filled the sky, some of them will actually stop and wonder if that's true."

As far as Kirchen can tell, his Tele is a late-'50s with a factory three-colour sunburst. "It's kind of like the story of the woodsman who's had the same axe in his family for six generations – but it's had five new heads and four new handles. Every single piece of metal on that guitar has been changed, save the six ferrules that the strings run through. They're original. But every peg, screw, wire, strap button … everything has been changed numerous times. Right now I have Joe Barden pickups in it, which I've had for quite a while, JT saddles, and a friend of mine carved me a new bridge out of a piece of steel.

"No matter what you do, though, to me it still sounds like a Telecaster," Kirchen concluded. "The thing that gets me is that no matter what I change on that guitar, the sound inherent to that body is always there."[97]

In 1992 Fender had a special Telecaster signed by a host of country stars and then presented it to President Bush (senior). But the real president of the Tele was honoured at a Rock & Roll Hall Of Fame ceremony the same year. Leo Fender was one of 12 music

Bashed-up relics from the time machine

▲ **1997 Fender HMT Acoustic-Electric**

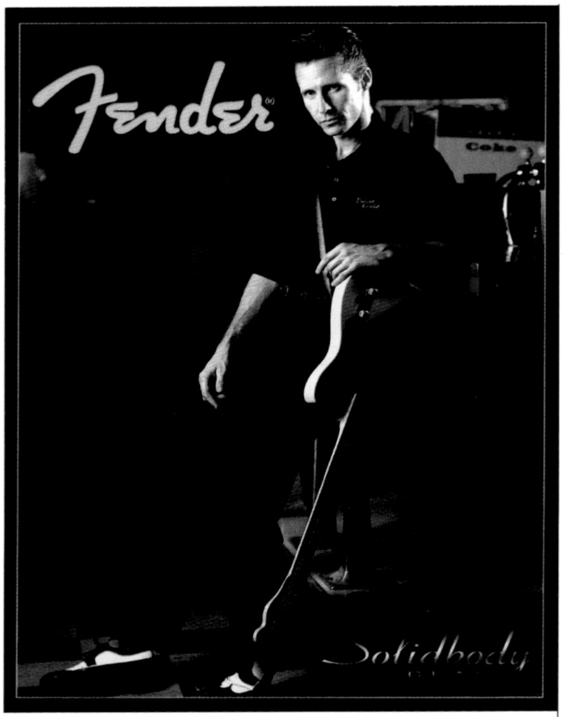

In 1995 Fender decided to market 'aged' new oldies; among the first releases was a '51 Nocaster (flyer, opposite, top). Today the Time Machine line includes models in three levels of ageing, including the 'bashed up' Relic style (main guitar). A further step into the past came in '96 on Fender's 50th anniversary with a limited edition of 50 Pine Telecaster & Amp sets (catalogue cover, opposite, below), the guitar re-creating the original Tele prototype. Another 1990s trend was the hybrid guitar, mixing regular magnetic and 'acoustic'-sounding piezo pickups. Fender's take on the idea came in the HMT models (far left). Influences on new musicians came not only from retro-styled catalogue shots (left) but from players such as Thom Yorke of Radiohead (right) who regularly used a 1970s humbucker'd Tele Deluxe.

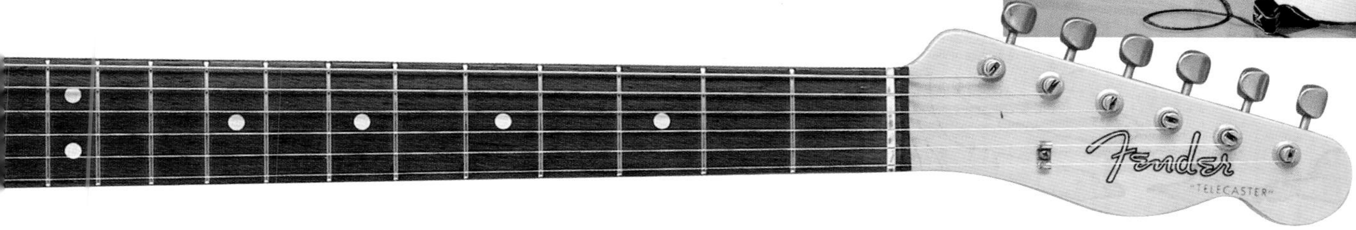

▲ **2001 Fender '63 Telecaster Relic lake placid blue**

legends inducted into the Hall that January, alongside Jimi Hendrix, Johnny Cash, and others. Leo's second wife Phyllis was there for Leo, who had died the previous year. "When I accepted his award I said that Leo truly believed that musicians were special angels, special envoys from the Lord," said Mrs Fender. "He believed he was put here to make the very best instruments in the world, because these special angels would help us get through this life, would ease our pain and ease our sadness, and help us celebrate."[98] Keith Richards also spoke on behalf of Leo, rather more prosaically. "He gave us the weapons," Richards told the Hall Of Fame gathering, leaving them with what he called the guitar players' prayer: "Caress it. Don't squeeze it."[99]

A bashed-up Relic from the Time Machine

Keith Richards was well aware of the power of Fender's past. A common request at the time from some artists was for the Custom Shop to make them a replica of a favourite old guitar, usually because the original was too valuable to risk taking out on the road. The story goes, according to a Fender insider, that Richards told the Shop that some replicas made for him for a Stones tour looked too new. "Bash 'em up a bit and I'll play 'em," he said. So the Shop began to include wear-and-tear distress marks to replicate the overall look of a battered old original. It was not a new idea, but certainly an effective one.

Then J.W. Black, the Fender Shop's Master Builder who had been working with the Stones, came up with the idea of offering these aged replicas as regular Custom Shop catalogued items, called Relics. "It started almost as a tongue-in-cheek thing," admitted John Page, "like worn-in Levis or something. It would look cool, and in the first three rows it'd look like you're playing a $20,000 Nocaster. But only you know that it's not really. That was how it started."

The Shop made two aged 1950s-era samples: a Nocaster (nickname for the transitional Broadcaster/Telecaster) and a 'Mary Kaye' Stratocaster (blond body, gold-plated parts). "We took them to the January 1995 NAMM trade show," recalled Page, "and put them under glass cases like they were pieces of art. Everyone came along and would say oh, that's really cool, you brought original ones as a tribute. And we were saying, er, yeah ... how many do you want? People went nuts! It was amazing."[100] Soon the Custom Shop was reacting to this new demand, offering a Relic Nocaster and three Relic Strats.

The line was expanded in 1998 by offering three strands of these 're-creations' in what is now known as the Time Machine series. There's the original Relic style, given 'aged' knocks and the look of heavy wear, as if the guitar has been out on the road for a generation or so; the Closet Classic, made to look as if it had been bought new way back when, played a few times, and then stuck in a closet; and N.O.S. (for 'New Old Stock'), as if an instrument had been bought brand new in the 1950s or 1960s and then put straight into a time machine that transported it to the present day. The kind of thing, in fact, that vintage guitar collectors and dealers regularly fantasise about, but which in real life rarely happens.

By 2005 the Custom Shop's Time Machine series included a '59 Esquire, a '51 Nocaster, and a '63 and '67 Telecaster, all available in the three different levels of aging, and listing around the $3,500 mark. This may seem a high price, but when you compare what you might have to pay now for good-condition originals – from about $5,000 or so for a '67 Tele to maybe $30,000 for a Nocaster – then the attraction becomes clearer.

And even if you could find originals at those prices, there's always the worry with a vintage piece about the veracity of this paint finish or that pickguard screw or those solder joints. The Time Machines at least take away any niggling doubts about originality. These Custom Shop specials obviously appeal to a relatively small but growing number of guitar fans, keen to acquire a new Fender with the feel and sound of an oldie, and in the case of the Relics made to look as if decades of wear-and-tear have stained the fingerboard, scuffed the body, and tarnished the hardware. The Time Machine series is a brilliant move, the nearest Fender has come with new instruments to the almost indefinable appeal of vintage guitars – which many thought was firmly and safely locked away in the past.

Fender marked its 50th anniversary in 1996. As you may recall from many pages back, in 1946 Leo Fender had parted company with his original partner, Doc Kauffman. Leo dissolved their K&F company and called his revised operation Fender Manufacturing, and then renamed it the Fender Electric Instrument Co in December 1947.

The modern company celebrated "50 Years of Excellence" in 1996 with some factory-made limited-edition anniversary models – the apparently timeless quartet of Telecaster, Precision Bass, Stratocaster, and Jazz Bass – each with a special commemorative neckplate. Fender also attached a 50th Anniversary decal to many products sold that year. The Custom Shop made some anniversary models too, notably 50 examples only of the Pine Telecaster & Amp set. The guitar recreated the original solidbody prototype with its steel-like headstock shape and angled control plate (and the amp was a replica of an early Model 26).

A big event for Fender in 1998 was the opening of a new factory in November, still in Corona, California. The company proudly described the impressive state-of-the-art plant as the world's most expensive and automated guitar factory. Since starting production at the original Corona factory back in 1985, Fender had grown to occupy a total of 115,000 square feet of space in ten buildings across the city. Such a rambling spread proved increasingly inefficient, and Fender began to plan a new centralised factory during the early 1990s. The new $20 million 177,000-square-feet plant affords a potentially growing production capacity for the future.

Some models were reorganised into new series in 1998, with new high-end U.S. models grouped as American Deluxes and reissues brought together as American Vintages. Fender had recognised from what was going on elsewhere in the marketplace that they had to move their quality up a notch. This upgrading led to the renaming of the American Standard series as the American Series in 2000.

The first Fenders with the company's new U.S.-made humbuckers had been the California 'Fat' models of 1997, including a Fat Tele with neck humbucker and Fat Strat

Bring on the humbucker revival

▲ 2005 Fender '72 Telecaster Deluxe

◂ **2000 Leo Fender Broadcaster**

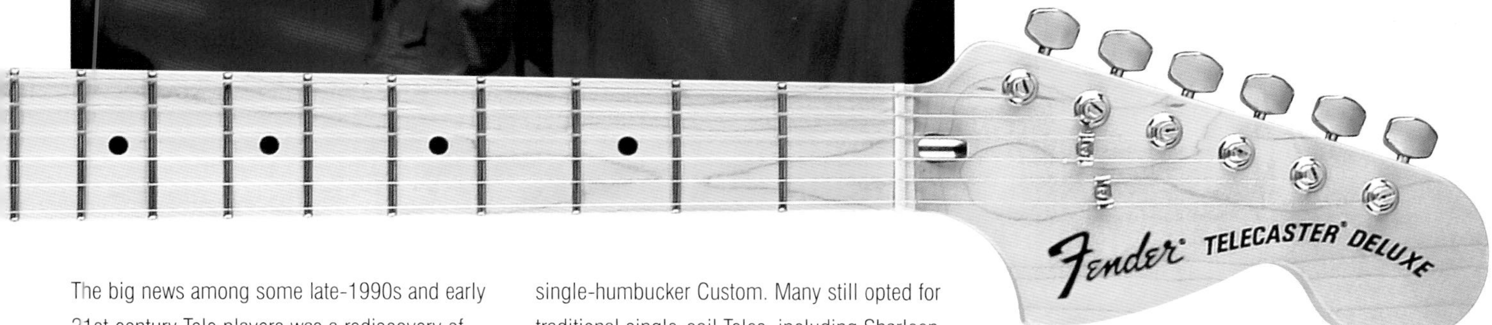

The big news among some late-1990s and early 21st century Tele players was a rediscovery of the humbucker-equipped models that originated in the 1970s. Among the popular models was the Deluxe, as played by Franz Ferdinand's mainman Alex Kapranos (opposite) and reissued by Fender in 2004 in a Mexican-made version (main guitar). Ian Ball of Gomez (above) opted for a humbucker'd f-hole Thinline, and that model too was reissued, in 1999, alongside the single-humbucker Custom. Many still opted for traditional single-coil Teles, including Sharleen Spiteri of Texas (strings ad, opposite). With the 50th anniversary in 2000 of the Telecaster's shortlived predecessor, the Broadcaster, the Custom Shop produced a limited-edition run of just 50 Leo Fender Broadcasters, with Leo's signature printed on the headstock in place of the usual logo.

with bridge 'bucker, but 2004 saw a new wave of stack-coil pickups, the Somarium Cobalt Noiseless (SCN) units designed by veteran pickup designer Bill Lawrence, as seen on American Deluxe and some American Series Telecasters. A new switching system, known as S-1, enhanced the new pickup capabilities.

It's always difficult to put the most recent music into any kind of context, and reporting on the state of current Tele popularity is no exception. What is clear is that at the time of writing there's a definite fashion for humbucker'd Teles among pop bands. The roots of this lie with Radiohead. Thom Yorke was seen regularly with a '70s two-humbucker Tele Deluxe, and on some live dates there would be the compelling sight of Yorke on Deluxe, Jonny Greenwood on a Tele Plus with bridge humbucker, and Ed O'Brien on a regular American Series Tele.

"MY TELE DELUXE IS A TOTALLY AMAZING GUITAR. IT'S STILL GOT THAT TELE SOUND, BUT IT DRIVES A LITTLE MORE."
Alex Kapranos, Franz Ferdinand

Radiohead's popularity cannot have done the idea of the humbucker'd Tele any harm. So we see members of Coldplay (Thinline), The Hives (Custom), Snow Patrol (Deluxe/Custom), Gomez (Thinline), Maroon 5 (Deluxe) and others queuing up to play them. Alex Kapranos of Franz Ferdinand opted for a Deluxe. "It's the one with a Stratocaster-type headstock and double humbuckers," explained the guitarist, "a totally amazing guitar. It's still got that Tele sound but it drives a little more. I play a lot of rhythmic stuff with my left hand and it picks up all the harmonic sounds from that, which other guitars really don't seem to. You can get some really strange sounds that you wouldn't expect to come from a guitar, I think probably because of those humbuckers."[101]

Into the future with a Telecaster close to hand

Fender reacted to the popularity of the old humbucker models – does this sound familiar? – and reissued the 1970s humbucker'd Teles as part of the Mexican-made Classic series: in 1999 along came the '72 Telecaster Custom (neck humbucker, bridge single-coil, four controls) and '72 Telecaster Thinline (f-hole, two humbuckers), and then in 2004 the '72 Telecaster Deluxe (two humbuckers, Strat-like headstock).

Many other guitarists continue to play regular single-coil Teles with equally profound musical effect, ranging from the coolest new pop band Bloc Party, whose Russell Lissack and Kele Okereke both favour classic Teles, to the hottest current Nashville twanger, Brent Mason, who's played with Shania Twain, Randy Travis and many, many more. Mason's heavily modified Tele brings us full circle, echoing the instrument's long and distinguished career in country's mainstream as well as the music's many backwaters and tributaries.

By 2005, Fender-branded Telecasters were organised by the company into ten series (other than Custom Shop instruments): Artist; American Vintage; American Deluxe; American Series; Highway 1; Classic; Deluxe; Limited Edition; Special Edition; and

Standard. Artist and Vintage are self-explanatory. American Deluxe models are deluxe versions of the American Series. Highway 1 models are reasonably-priced U.S.-made guitars, with some involvement from the Mexico factory. Classic models are Mexico-made vintage-style guitars; Deluxe models are deluxe versions of Mexico's Standard series. Limited Editions and Special Editions cover various other models, at the time of writing apparently still coming from Japan.

The Squier brand offered some interesting Telecasters in the first years of the 21st century, such as the Double Fat Tele Deluxe of 2001, with carved mahogany body, two exposed-coil humbuckers, and metallic finishes, and the Master Series that includes the Chambered Tele and Thinline Tele HH with their set necks, twin humbuckers, and Les Paul-style control layouts. The impression here was that Fender perhaps felt more able to experiment away from their main brand.

With so many different models, it can be daunting trying to find your way around the Fender lines. At the time of writing, Fender's pricelist had no fewer than 43 different Fender-brand Telecasters (including a few Esquires and Nocasters) plus eight Squiers. They ranged in list-price from a Squier Affinity Tele at $282.99 to a Fender Merle Haggard Signature Telecaster for $6,256.99. Fender defended the vast array in the 2005 catalogue: "So, why do we make so many models of Fender electric guitars? Because there are so many different styles of music, and even more individual artists playing them!" Fair point: but with all that choice – and often with nothing more on the guitar than "Fender" and "Telecaster" – it can sometimes be tricky to know for sure what you're looking at. For example, you might be buying a secondhand guitar – an area of the market where people have been known to blur the truth.

LEO FENDER LOVED FEW THINGS MORE THAN GADGETS, AND WOULD HAVE BEEN ENTHRALLED BY THE LATEST FENDER FACTORY

But how can Fender do otherwise? Of course they have to acknowledge that rich and colourful history, which as we've seen is just full to the brim with great guitars and even greater players. But it's you they need to keep an eye on: the players of today and the players of tomorrow.

Fender's Corona, California, factory may be some 20 miles from Fullerton and Leo Fender's original workshops, but it's a universe away from the humble steel shacks that were the first home for Fender production and the birthplace of the earliest Esquires and Broadcasters and Telecasters, back at the turn of the 1950s. Leo loved few things more than gadgets, and would have been enthralled by the new plant – not least its automated conveyors that shift an enormous inventory of guitar components from storage area to production line. But Leo would be looking most keenly at what tomorrow might bring. That pickup over there. Yes, that one. Surely we could make it sound just a little bit better. Couldn't we?

Brand new style or classic retro vibe?

The most recent Fender lines offer Teles with a mix of new ideas alongside established traditional-style instruments. So we get a 21st-century take on humbucker-equipped Teles in an ad for the HH and HS models (below) or this American Deluxe (main guitar) with a pair of 'buckers on board and fine enough timber and finish to tempt many a Gibson or PRS fan. Much more down to earth is the Mexican-made Standard (right), pictured in the lefty option. Another ad (opposite) highlights the latest American series, including the vintage-style Ash model. New players such as Bloc Party's Kele Okereke (right) are still drawn to the Tele's timeless appeal, while the '59 Esquire Relic (below) shows that some of us are still prepared to pay for classic styling and a careworn look.

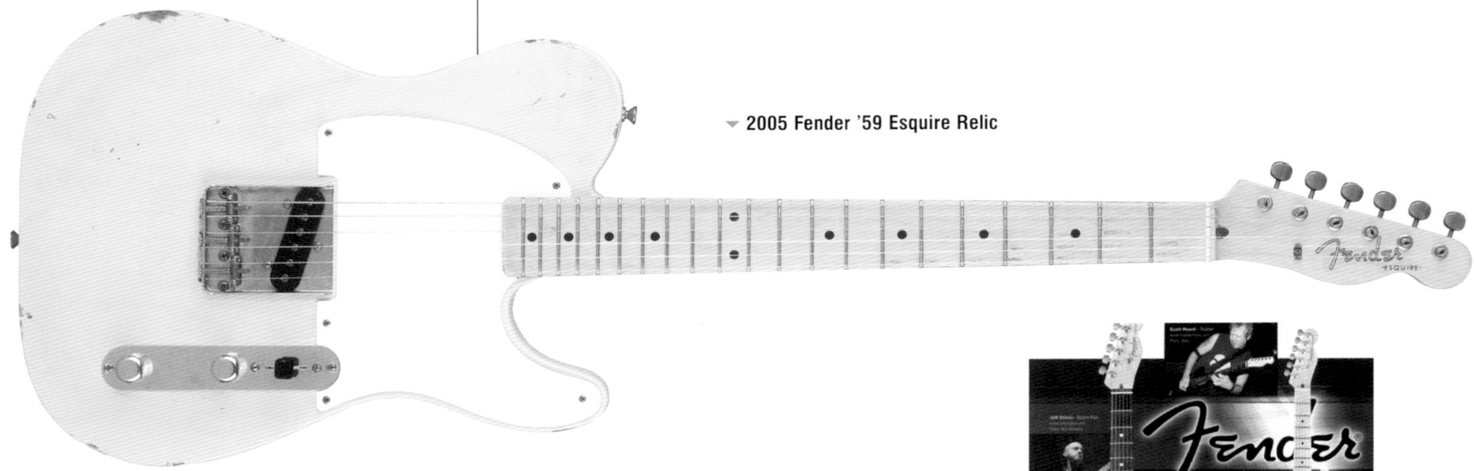

2005 Fender '59 Esquire Relic

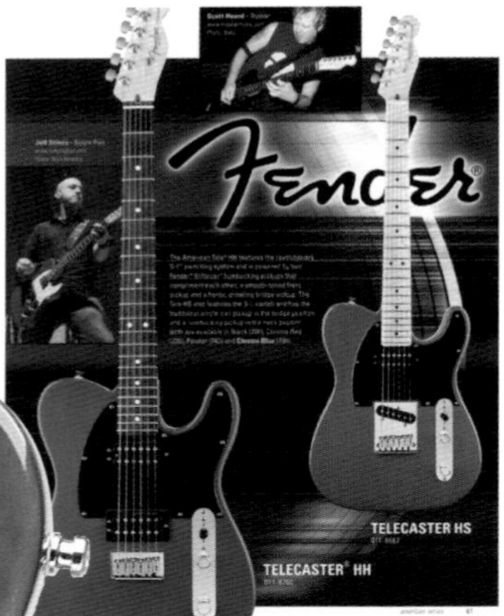

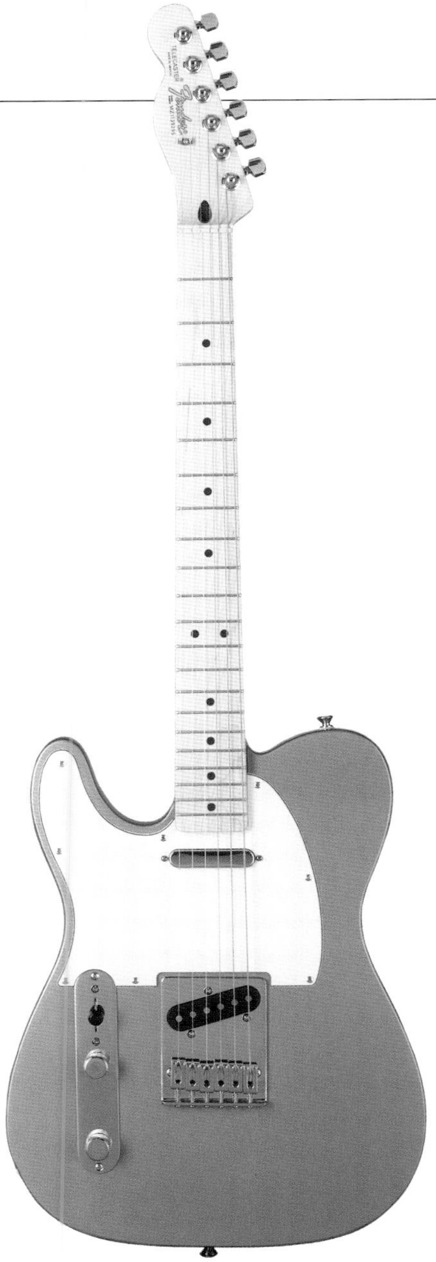

▲ 2003 Fender Standard Telecaster sage green

▲ 2004 Fender American Deluxe Telecaster QMT bing cherry transparent

Endnotes

1. Author's interview April 29th 2005
2. *Guitar Player* April 1995
3. Author's interview February 6th 1992
4. *Guitar Player* October 1982
5. Author's interview February 10th 1992
6. *Bay Area Music* August 29th 1980
7. Author's interview with Karl Olmsted February 5th 1992
8. *Guitar Player* September 1971
9. Author's interview February 5th 1992
10. Author's interview February 8th 1992
11. Author's interview February 10th 1992
12. Author's interview with Forrest White February 5th 1992
13. Author's interview February 10th 1992
14. Author's interview February 5th 1992
15. *Daily News Tribune* November 8th 1949
16. *Washington Post* December 17th 1972
17. Author's interview February 10th 1992
18. *Guitar Player* September 1971
19. Author's interview with Bill Carson September 6th 1991
20. Author's interview February 8th 1992
21. Author's interview February 8th 1992
22. *Fender Catalogue No.2* 1950
23. Author's interview February 10th 1992
24. Author's interview February 10th 1992
25. *Guitar Player* December 1984
26. Author's interview February 10th 1992
27. Author's interview February 8th 1992
28. Author's interview February 8th 1992
29. Author's interview February 10th 1992
30. *Guitar Player* July 1979
31. Author's interview with Dale Hyatt February 10th 1992
32. *Los Angeles Times* April 3rd 1955
33. *The Music Trades* June 1953
34. Author's interview February 5th 1992
35. Author's interview February 5th 1992
36. Author's interview February 5th 1992
37. Author's interview February 5th 1992
38. Author's interview April 29th 2005
39. *Melody Maker* September 8th 1956
40. *Melody Maker* October 25th 1958
41. *Guitar Player* August 1983
42. Author's interview February 8th 1992
43. Author's interview February 10th 1992
44. Author's interview February 5th 1992
45. Author's interview February 10th 1992
46. *The Music Trades* January 1965
47. *The Music Trades* January 1965
48. *International Musician* August 1978
49. Author's interview February 10th 1992
50. Author's interview February 5th 1992
51. Author's interview February 8th 1992
52. Author's interview February 10th 1992
53. Author's interview February 10th 1992
54. Richard Smith *Fender: The Sound Heard 'Round The World* (Garfish 1995)
55. Author's interview February 5th 1992
56. *Melody Maker* June 25th 1966
57. *Beat Instrumental* October 1967
58. Author's interview July 10th 2003
59. Author's interview April 27th 2005
60. Author's interview February 8th 1992
61. Author's interview April 29th 2005
62. Author's interview February 10th 1992
63. Author's interview February 10th 1992
64. Author's interview February 8th 1992
65. *Guitar Player* April 1983
66. Author's interview April 27th 2005
67. *Guitar Player* October 1976
68. Steve Howe with Tony Bacon *The Steve Howe Guitar Collection* (Balafon 1994)
69. Author's interview August 31st 1981
70. Author's interview October 30th 1992
71. *Guitar Player* October 1976
72. *Rolling Stone* April 1st 1999
73. *Syracuse Herald* June 29th 1986
74. *Washington Post* December 17th 1972
75. *Guitar Player* September 1983
76. *Guitar Player* December 1976
77. Author's interview February 5th 1992
78. Author's interview February 4th 1992
79. Author's interview June 2nd 2005
80. *Guitar Player* May 1978
81. Author's interview February 4th 1992
82. Author's interview June 2nd 2005
83. Author's interview February 4th 1992
84. *Guitar Trader Vintage Guitar Bulletin* Vol.2 No.7 July 1983
85. Author's interview February 4th 1992
86. Author's interview February 4th 1992
87. *Guitar Player* May 1981
88. Author's interview April 12th 2005
89. *San Francisco Chronicle* January 15th 1985
90. Author's interview February 11th 1985
91. Author's interview June 2nd 2005
92. Author's interview December 2nd 1997
93. Author's interview April 29th 2005
94. Author's interview April 27th 2005
95. Author's interview June 2nd 2005
96. *The Guitar Magazine* March 1999
97. Author's interview April 12th 2005
98. Author's interview February 6th 1992
99. *New York Times* January 16th 1992
100. Author's interview December 2nd 1997
101. *The Guitar Magazine* April 2004

Reference Section

How to use the **reference listing**

The main Reference listing offers a simple, condensed format to convey a large amount of information about every Fender Telecaster and Esquire (and related models) made between 1950 and 2005. The notes here are intended to ensure that you gain the most from this unique inventory.

The list covers all the production Fender-brand models made by Fender US between 1950 and 2005, the output of Fender Mexico between 1991 and 2005, the export models of Fender Japan issued since 1982 until 2005, and the few Fender-brand models made in Korea between 1992 and 2005. Models by Squier and other Fender-related brands are not included.

The listings

The five main sections within the Reference Listing are: US-made Telecasters; Mexican-made Telecasters; Japanese-made Telecasters; Korean-made Telecasters; and a few brief paragraphs about Squier. Each model is listed under the various headings by the alphabetical order of its model name. Where a model name is also a person's name, the first word still supplies the alphabetical order. For example, the Jerry Donahue Telecaster is listed under J, not D. The exception to alphabetical order is found under the US 'Regular' grouping where the models are shown in chronological order for ease of reference.

Reading the entries

At the head of each entry in the main listings is the model name in bold type, followed in italics by a date or range of dates showing the production period of the instrument. It's worth stressing here that these dates are approximate. In many cases it's virtually impossible to pinpoint with total accuracy the period during which a model was in production at the factory. For example, Fender's dated promo material does not always reflect what was being made at that precise time. Naturally our extensive research has resulted in the most accurate dates possible – but please treat them as approximate, because that is all they can be.

Following the model name and production date(s) is a brief one-sentence identification of the guitar in question, intended to help you recognise a specific model at a glance. To enable you to do this we have noted elements of the guitar's design that are unique to that particular model.

For some guitars there may be a sentence that reads "Similar to ... except:", which will refer to another model entry and then itemise any differences between the two.

Common features

To avoid repetition, we have considered a number of features to be common to all models, and these are not shown in the main listings. You can always presume the following:

- Metal tuner buttons unless stated.
- Standard Fender headstock shape unless stated.
- Four-screw neckplate unless stated.
- Bolt-on neck unless stated.
- 25½-inch scale, 21 frets unless stated.
- Fingerboards with dot markers unless stated.
- Single-coil pickups unless stated.
- Nickel- or chrome-plated hardware unless stated.

Specification points

In the main model entries there are a series of bullet points. This list of specification points, separated into groups, provides details of the particular model's features. In the order listed the points refer to:

- Neck, fingerboard, headstock.
- Body.
- Pickups.
- Controls.
- Pickguard.
- Bridge.
- Hardware finish.

Of course, not every model will need all seven points. Some models were made in a number of variations, and where applicable these are listed (beginning *Also...*) after the specification points. Any other general comments are made in this position, and a Custom Shop general production model is identified as such here.

Some models have only a short listing. This is often because they are based on an earlier guitar. These listings usually refer you to the entry for the original instrument.

Generally excluded from the listings are models that do not include 'Telecaster', 'Esquire' or 'Broadcaster' somewhere on the instrument.

All this information is designed to tell you more about your Fender guitar. By using the general information and illustrations contained earlier in *Six Decades Of The Fender Telecaster*, combined with the knowledge obtained from the unique reference section that follows, you should be able to build up a very full picture of your instrument and its pedigree.

US-MADE TELECASTERS

US Telecasters are divided into five sections: REGULAR; REPLICA; REVISED; OTHER; CUSTOM SHOP.

Regular Telecasters

Listed here in chronological order are the standard versions of the Telecaster.

TELECASTER *1951-83* 21 frets, slab single-cutaway body, two single-coils, three-saddle bridge.

- Fretted maple neck (1951-59 and 1969-83), maple neck with rosewood fingerboard (1959-83), maple fingerboard official option (1967-69); truss-rod adjuster at body end; one string-guide (two from 1972).
- Slab single-cutaway body; originally blond only, later sunburst or colours.
- One plain metal-cover pickup (at neck) and one black six-polepiece pickup (angled in bridgeplate).
- Two controls (volume, tone; but originally volume, pickup blender) and three-way selector, all on metal plate adjoining pickguard; side-mounted jack socket.
- Five-screw (eight-screw from 1959) black plastic pickguard (white plastic from 1954; white laminated plastic 1963-75 and 1981-83; black laminated plastic 1975-81).
- Three-saddle raised-sides bridge with through-body stringing (strings anchored at bridgeplate and not through body 1958-60).

■ Previously known as **BROADCASTER** (1950-51), but some transitional examples have no model name on the headstock, unofficially known as **NOCASTER**.
■ Fender Bigsby bridge and vibrato tailpiece option (1967-74), no through-body string holes if unit factory-fitted.
■ Also **CUSTOM TELECASTER**, with bound body (1959-72).
■ Also **PAISLEY RED TELECASTER**, with red paisley-pattern body finish and clear plastic pickguard (1968-69).
■ Also **BLUE FLOWER TELECASTER**, with blue floral-pattern body finish and clear plastic pickguard (1968-69).
■ Also **ROSEWOOD TELECASTER**, with fretted rosewood neck, solid (later semi-solid) rosewood body and black laminated plastic pickguard (1969-72).
■ Also **ANTIGUA TELECASTER**, with white/brown shaded body finish and matching-colour laminated plastic pickguard (1977-79).
■ Also **INTERNATIONAL COLOR TELECASTER**, with special colour finishes, white laminated plastic pickguard and black-plated pickguard screws (1981).

TELECASTER STANDARD *1983-84* 21 frets, slab single-cutaway body, two single-coils, six-saddle bridge/tailpiece.

- Fretted maple neck; truss-rod adjuster at headstock end; two string-guides.
- Slab single-cutaway body; sunburst or colours.
- One plain metal-cover pickup at neck and one black six-polepiece pickup (angled in bridgeplate).
- Two controls (volume, tone) & three-way selector, all on metal plate by pickguard; side-mounted jack socket.
- Five-screw (originally eight-screw) white plastic pickguard.
- Six-saddle flat bridge/tailpiece (no through-body stringing).

■ Also in red, yellow or blue streaked finish, unofficially known as **BOWLING BALL** or **MARBLE** Telecaster (1984).

AMERICAN ASH TELECASTER See later **AMERICAN STANDARD** listing

AMERICAN TELECASTER See later **AMERICAN STANDARD** listing

AMERICAN STANDARD TELECASTER *1988-2000* 22 frets, slab single-cutaway body, two single-coils, six-saddle bridge.

- Fretted maple neck or maple neck with rosewood fingerboard; 22 frets; truss-rod adjuster at headstock end; one string-guide.
- Slab single-cutaway body; sunburst or colours.
- One plain metal-cover pickup with visible height-adjustment screws (at neck) and one black six-polepiece pickup (angled in bridgeplate).
- Two controls (volume, tone) and three-way selector, all on metal plate adjoining pickguard; side-mounted jack socket.
- Eight-screw white laminated plastic pickguard.
- Six-saddle flat bridge with through-body stringing (earliest examples with raised-sides type).

■ Also with anodised aluminium hollow body option (1994-95).
■ Also **AMERICAN ASH TELECASTER** (2004-current).
■ Known as **AMERICAN TELECASTER** (2001-current).

Replica Telecasters

Listed in alphabetical order here are the models based on various Regular Telecasters and that we term 'replicas'.

'52 TELECASTER *1982-84 and 1986-current* Replica of 1952-period original (see **TELECASTER** listing in earlier Regular Telecasters section).

'52 TELE SPECIAL *1999-2001* Replica of 1952-period original (see **TELECASTER** listing in earlier Regular Telecasters section). Body sunburst only, gold-plated hardware.

50s TELECASTER *1996-98* Replica of 1950s-period original (see **TELECASTER** listing in earlier Regular Telecasters section). Gold-plated hardware option. Custom Shop production.

60s TELECASTER CUSTOM *1996-98* Replica of 1960s-period original (see **TELECASTER** listing in earlier Regular

Telecasters section). Gold-plated hardware option. Custom Shop production.

'60 TELECASTER CUSTOM *2003-04* Replica of 1960s-period original (see **TELECASTER** listing in earlier Regular Telecasters section). Available in N.O.S, Closet Classic and Relic versions. Custom Shop production.

'62 TELECASTER CUSTOM *1999-current* Replica of 1960s-period original (see **TELECASTER** listing in earlier Regular Telecasters section).

'63 TELECASTER *1999-current* Replica of 1960s-period original (see **TELECASTER** listing in earlier Regular Telecasters section). Available in N.O.S., Closet Classic and Relic versions. This model is Custom Shop production.

'67 TELECASTER *2004-current* Replica of 1967-period original (see **TELECASTER** listing in earlier Regular Telecasters section). Available in N.O.S., Closet Classic and Relic versions. Custom Shop production.

Revised Telecasters

Listed here are what we term 'revised' models, adapted versions of the basic Regular Telecasters.

ALBERT COLLINS TELECASTER *1990-current* Signature on headstock.

- Maple neck with maple fingerboard; truss-rod adjuster at body end; one string-guide; Albert Collins signature on headstock.
- Slab single-cutaway bound body; natural only.
- One metal-cover six-polepiece humbucker pickup (at neck) and one black six-polepiece pickup (angled in bridgeplate).
- Two controls (volume, tone) and three-way selector, all on metal plate adjoining pickguard; side-mounted jack socket.
- Eight-screw white laminated plastic pickguard.
- Six-saddle raised-sides bridge with through-body stringing.

■ Custom Shop production.

ALUMINUM-BODY TELECASTER *1994-95* Anodised aluminium hollow-body option on **AMERICAN STANDARD TELECASTER** (see listing in earlier Regular Telecasters section).

AMERICAN CLASSIC TELECASTER first version *1995-98* Three pickups (two white, one black), inverted control plate.
Similar to **AMERICAN STANDARD TELECASTER** (see listing in earlier Regular Telecasters section), except:

- Two white six-polepiece pickups and one black six-polepiece pickup (angled in bridgeplate).
- Two controls (volume, tone) and five-way selector, all on inverted metal plate adjoining pickguard.
- Eight-screw white pearl or tortoiseshell laminated plastic pickguard.

■ Gold-plated hardware option.
■ Custom Shop production.

AMERICAN CLASSIC TELECASTER second version *1999-2000* Two pickups, inverted control plate.
Similar to **AMERICAN CLASSIC TELECASTER first version** (see earlier listing), except:

- One plain metal-cover pickup with visible height-adjustment screws (at neck) and one black six-polepiece pickup (angled in bridgeplate).
- Two controls (volume, tone) and three-way selector (four-way from 2003), all on inverted metal plate adjoining pickguard.

■ Custom Shop production.
■ Known as **CUSTOM CLASSIC TELECASTER** (2000-current).

AMERICAN DELUXE ASH TELECASTER See later **AMERICAN DELUXE TELECASTER third version** listing

AMERICAN DELUXE POWER TELE *2000-01* Bound body, two dual-concentric controls.
Similar to **AMERICAN DELUXE TELECASTER second version** (see later listing), except:

- Two dual-concentric controls (volume, tone for magnetic and piezo pickups), three-way selector and mini-switch, all on metal plate adjoining pickguard.
- Fishman Power Bridge with six piezo-pickup saddles.

■ Previously available as option on **AMERICAN DELUXE TELECASTER second version** (1999-2000).

AMERICAN DELUXE TELECASTER first version *1998-99* Bound body, 22 frets, additional centre pickup.
Similar to **AMERICAN STANDARD TELECASTER** (see listing in earlier Regular Telecasters section), except:

- Bound body.
- Centre position white six-polepiece pickup.
- Two controls (volume, tone), five-way selector and mini-switch, all on metal plate adjoining pickguard.
- Eight-screw white or tortoiseshell laminated plastic pickguard.

AMERICAN DELUXE TELECASTER second version *1999-2004* Bound body, 22 frets.
Similar to **AMERICAN DELUXE TELECASTER first version** (see earlier listing), except:

- One plain metal-cover pickup with visible height-adjustment screws (at neck) and one black six-polepiece pickup (angled in bridgeplate).
- Two controls (volume, tone) and three-way selector, all on metal plate adjoining pickguard.

■ Also with optional Fishman Power

Bridge, with piezo-pickup bridge saddles, two dual-concentric controls, three-way selector and mini-switch (1999-2000). Known as **AMERICAN DELUXE POWER TELE** (2000-01).

AMERICAN DELUXE TELECASTER third version *2004-current* Bound body, 22 frets, volume control with push-switch.
Similar to **AMERICAN DELUXE TELECASTER first version** (see earlier listing), except:
- One plain metal-cover pickup with visible height-adjustment screws (at neck) and one black six-polepiece pickup (angled in bridgeplate).
- Two controls (volume with push-switch, tone) and three-way selector, all on metal plate adjoining pickguard.
- Eight-screw laminated plastic pickguard in various colours.

■ Also **AMERICAN DELUXE ASH TELECASTER**, with ash body (2004-current).

AMERICAN DELUXE TELECASTER FMT *2004-current* Flame maple top, two humbuckers, no pickguard.
- Maple neck with ebony fingerboard; 22 frets; truss-rod adjuster at headstock end; one string-guide.
- Single-cutaway body with flame maple top; various colours.
- Two black coverless humbuckers.
- Two controls (volume with push-switch, tone) and three-way selector, all on body; side-mounted jack socket.
- No pickguard.
- Six-saddle small bridge with through-body stringing.

■ Also **AMERICAN DELUXE TELECASTER QMT**, with quilted maple top (2004-current).

AMERICAN DELUXE TELECASTER QMT See previous listing

AMERICAN FAT TELE See later **U.S. FAT TELE** listing.

AMERICAN STANDARD B-BENDER TELECASTER *1995-98* Standard Tele pickup layout, 22 frets, B-Bender string-bending device installed.
Similar to **AMERICAN STANDARD TELECASTER** (see listing in earlier Regular Telecasters section), except:
- Fretted maple neck only.
- Factory-fitted B-Bender built-in bending device for 2nd string.

AMERICAN TELECASTER HS *2003-current* Humbucker at neck, no pickguard.
- Fretted maple neck or maple neck with rosewood fingerboard; 22 frets; truss-rod adjuster at headstock end; one string-guide.
- Slab single-cutaway body; various colours.
- One black coverless humbucker (at neck) and one black six-polepiece pickup (angled in bridgeplate).
- Two controls (volume, tone) and three-way selector, all on metal plate; side-mounted jack socket.
- No pickguard.
- Six-saddle flat bridge with through-body stringing.

AMERICAN TELECASTER HH *2003-current* Two humbuckers, no pickguard.
Similar to **AMERICAN TELECASTER HS** (see earlier listing), except:
- Two black coverless humbuckers.
- Six-saddle small bridge with through-body stringing.

ANTIGUA TELECASTER See **TELECASTER** listing in earlier Regular Telecasters section.

ANTIGUA TELECASTER CUSTOM See later **TELECASTER CUSTOM** listing.

ANTIGUA TELECASTER DELUXE See later **TELECASTER DELUXE** listing.

BAJO SEXTO TELECASTER *1992-98* Model name is shown on headstock, extended-scale neck, 24 frets.
- Fretted maple neck; 767mm (30.2") scale, 24 frets; truss-rod adjuster at body end; one string-guide; Bajo Sexto on headstock.
- Slab single-cutaway body; sunburst or blond.
- One plain metal-cover pickup (at neck) and one black six-polepiece pickup (angled in bridgeplate).
- Two controls (volume, tone) and three-way selector, all on metal plate adjoining pickguard; side-mounted jack socket.
- Five-screw black plastic pickguard.
- Three-saddle raised-sides bridge with through-body stringing.

■ Custom Shop production.

B-BENDER TELECASTER See earlier **AMERICAN STANDARD B-BENDER TELECASTER** listing.

BLACK & GOLD TELECASTER *1981-83* Normal Tele pickup layout, 21 frets, black body, gold hardware.
Similar to 1981-period **TELECASTER** (see listing in earlier Regular Telecasters section), except:
- Black-face headstock.
- Body black only.
- Black laminated plastic pickguard.
- Six-saddle heavy-duty small bridge with through-body stringing.
- Gold-plated brass hardware.

BLUE FLOWER TELECASTER See **TELECASTER** listing in earlier Regular Telecasters section.

BOWLING BALL TELECASTER (also unofficially known as Marble Telecaster) See **TELECASTER STANDARD** listing in earlier Regular Telecasters section.

CALIFORNIA FAT TELE *1997-98* "California Series" on headstock, one humbucker and one single-coil.
- Fretted maple neck; truss-rod adjuster at headstock end; one

string-guide; "California Series" on headstock.
- Slab single-cutaway body; sunburst or colours.
- One metal-cover six-polepiece humbucker (at neck) and one black six-polepiece pickup (angled in bridgeplate).
- Two controls (volume, tone) and three-way selector, all on metal plate adjoining pickguard; side-mounted jack socket.
- Eight-screw white laminated plastic pickguard.
- Six-saddle raised-sides bridge with through-body stringing.

CALIFORNIA TELE *1997-98* "California Series" on headstock, two single-coils.
Similar to **CALIFORNIA FAT TELE**, except:
- Fretted maple neck, or maple neck with rosewood fingerboard.
- One white six-polepiece pickup (at neck) and one black six-polepiece pickup (angled in bridgeplate).

CLARENCE WHITE TELECASTER *1993-2001* Signature on headstock.
- Fretted maple neck; truss-rod adjuster at body end; Scruggs Peg banjo-style de-tuners for 1st and 6th strings; Clarence White signature on headstock.
- Slab single-cutaway body; sunburst only.
- One white six-polepiece pickup (at neck) and one black six-polepiece pickup (angled in bridgeplate).
- Two controls (volume, tone) and three-way selector, all on metal plate adjoining pickguard; side-mounted jack socket.
- Eight-screw tortoiseshell laminated plastic pickguard.
- Three-saddle raised-sides bridge with through-body stringing; factory-fitted B-Bender built-in bending device for 2nd string.

■ Custom Shop production.

CUSTOM CLASSIC TELECASTER See earlier **AMERICAN CLASSIC TELECASTER second version** listing.

CUSTOM TELECASTER See **TELECASTER** listing in earlier Regular Telecasters section.

DANNY GATTON TELECASTER *1990-current* Signature on headstock.
- Fretted maple neck; 22 frets; truss-rod adjuster at body end; one string-guide; Danny Gatton signature on headstock.
- Slab single-cutaway body; blond or gold.
- Two black twin-blade pickups (bridgeplate pickup angled).
- Two controls (volume, tone) and three-way selector, all on metal plate adjoining pickguard; side-mounted jack socket.
- Five-screw cream plastic pickguard.
- Modified three-saddle raised-sides bridge with through-body stringing.

■ Custom Shop production.

DELUXE TELECASTER PLUS See later **TELECASTER PLUS** listing.

ELITE TELECASTER *1983-84* Two white plain-top pickups.
- Fretted maple neck, or maple neck with rosewood fingerboard; truss-rod adjuster at headstock end; two string-guides.
- Slab single-cutaway bound body; sunburst or colours.
- Two white plain-top humbucker pickups.
- Four controls (two volume, two tone) and three-way selector, all on body; side-mounted jack socket; active circuit.
- White laminated plastic optional mini pickguard.
- Redesigned six-saddle bridge/tailpiece.

■ Also **GOLD ELITE TELECASTER**, with pearl tuner buttons and gold-plated hardware (1983-84).

■ Also **WALNUT ELITE TELECASTER**, with walnut neck and ebony fingerboard, walnut body, pearl tuner buttons and gold-plated hardware (1983-84).

FLAT HEAD TELECASTER *2004-current* Crossed piston inlay at 12th fret.
- Maple neck with ebony fingerboard; 22 frets; truss-rod adjuster at body end; one string-guide; crossed piston inlay at 12th fret.
- Single-cutaway body; various colours.
- Two black plain-top humbuckers.
- One control (volume) and three-way selector, all on body; side-mounted jack socket.
- No pickguard.
- Six-saddle small bridge with through-body stringing.
- Black-plated hardware.

■ Custom Shop production.

GOLD ELITE TELECASTER See earlier **ELITE TELECASTER** listing.

HIGHWAY 1 TELECASTER *2003-current* Satin finish, 22 frets.
- Fretted maple neck, or maple neck with rosewood fingerboard; 22 frets; truss-rod adjuster at headstock end; one string-guide.
- Slab single-cutaway body; satin sunburst or colours.
- One plain metal-cover pickup (at neck) and one black six-polepiece pickup (angled in bridgeplate).
- Two controls (volume, tone) and three-way selector, all on metal plate adjoining pickguard; side-mounted jack socket.
- Five-screw white plastic pickguard.
- Three-saddle raised-sides bridge with through-body stringing.

HIGHWAY 1 TEXAS TELECASTER 2004-current Satin finish, 21 frets.
Similar to **HIGHWAY 1 TELECASTER** (see previous listing), except:

- Fretted maple neck only; 21 frets.
- Satin sunburst or blonde.

INTERNATIONAL COLOR TELECASTER See TELECASTER listing in earlier Regular Telecasters section.

JAMES BURTON TELECASTER *1990-current* Signature on headstock.
- Fretted maple neck; truss-rod adjuster at body end; one string-guide; James Burton signature on headstock.
- Slab single-cutaway body; black with gold or red paisley-pattern, red or white.
- Three black plain-top Lace Sensor pickups (bridge pickup angled).
- Two controls (volume, tone) and five-way selector, all on metal plate; side-mounted jack socket.
- No pickguard.
- Six-saddle small bridge with through-body stringing.
- Black-plated or gold-plated hardware.

JERRY DONAHUE TELECASTER *1992-2001* Signature on headstock.
- Fretted maple neck; truss-rod adjuster at body end; one string-guide; Jerry Donahue signature on headstock.
- Slab single-cutaway body; sunburst or colours.
- Two black six-polepiece pickups (bridgeplate pickup angled).
- Two controls (volume, tone) and five-way selector, all on metal plate adjoining pickguard; side-mounted jack socket.
- Five-screw black laminated plastic pickguard.
- Three-saddle raised-sides bridge with through-body stringing.
- Gold-plated hardware.

■ Custom Shop production.

JIMMY BRYANT TELECASTER *2004-current* Decorative tooled leather pickguard overlay.
- Fretted maple neck; truss-rod adjuster at body end; one string-guide.
- Slab single-cutaway body; blonde only.
- One plain metal-cover pickup (at neck) and one black six-polepiece pickup (angled in bridgeplate).
- Two controls (volume, tone) and three-way selector, all on metal plate adjoining pickguard; side-mounted jack socket.
- Five-screw black plastic pickguard with decorative tooled leather overlay.
- Three-saddle raised sides bridge with through-body stringing.

■ Custom Shop production.

JOHN JORGENSON TELECASTER *1998-2001* Signature on headstock.
- Maple neck with rosewood or ebony fingerboard; 22 frets; truss-rod adjuster at headstock end; no string-guide; locking tuners; John Jorgenson signature on headstock.
- Slab single-cutaway bound body; black or sparkle colours.
- Two plain metal-cover pickups (at neck) and two black six-polepiece pickups (angled in bridgeplate).
- Two controls (volume, tone) and five-way selector, all on metal plate adjoining pickguard; side-mounted jack socket.
- Eight-screw clear plastic pickguard.
- Three-saddle raised-sides bridge with through-body stringing.

■ Custom Shop production.

J5:HB TELECASTER *2003-current* Headstock with three tuners each side, humbucker at bridge.
- Maple neck with rosewood fingerboard; 22 frets; truss-rod adjuster at headstock end; no string-guide; three tuners each side.
- Slab single-cutaway bound body; black only.
- One plain metal-cover pickup with visible height adjustment screws (at neck) and one black coverless humbucker (in bridgeplate).
- Two controls (volume, tone) on metal plate adjoining pickguard, three-way selector on body ; side-mounted jack socket.
- Eight-screw chromed pickguard.
- Six-saddle flat bridge with through-body stringing.

■ Custom Shop production.

J5:BIGSBY *2003-current* Headstock with three tuners each side, Bigsby vibrato tailpiece.
Similar to **J5:HB TELECASTER** (see earlier listing), except:
- One plain metal-cover pickup with visible height-adjustment screws (at neck) and one black six-polepiece pickup (angled in bridgeplate).
- Two controls (volume, tone) on metal plate adjoining pickguard.
- Six-saddle bridge, separate Bigsby vibrato tailpiece.

MARBLE TELECASTER (also known unofficially as Bowling Ball Telecaster) See **TELECASTER STANDARD** listing in earlier Regular Telecasters section.

MERLE HAGGARD TELE *1997-current* Signature on headstock.
- Fretted maple neck; 22 frets; truss-rod adjuster at body end; one string-guide; pearl tuner buttons; "Tuff Dog Tele" inlay and Merle Haggard signature on headstock.
- Slab single-cutaway bound body; sunburst only.
- One plain metal-cover pickup (at neck) and one black six-polepiece pickup (angled in bridgeplate).
- Two controls (volume, tone) and four-way selector, all on metal plate adjoining pickguard; side-mounted jack socket.
- Seven-screw cream plastic re-styled pickguard.
- Six-saddle flat bridge with through-body stringing.
- Gold-plated hardware.

■ Custom Shop production.

■ Catalogue name varies: Merle Haggard Tribute Tuff Dog Tele (1997-2000); Merle Haggard Tribute Tele (2001-2003); Merle Haggard Signature Telecaster (2004-current).

NASHVILLE B-BENDER TELE *1998-current* Additional centre pickup, B-Bender string-bending device installed.
Similar to **AMERICAN STANDARD B-BENDER TELECASTER**, except:
- Centre-position white six-polepiece pickup.
- Five-way selector.
- Eight-screw white pearloid laminated plastic pickguard.

PAISLEY RED TELECASTER See TELECASTER listing in earlier Regular Telecasters section.

ROSEWOOD TELECASTER See TELECASTER listing in earlier Regular Telecasters section.

SET NECK TELE JNR *1995-99* Two large black rectangular pickups.
- Mahogany glued-in neck with pao ferro fingerboard; 22 frets; truss-rod adjuster at headstock end; one string-guide; neck and headstock face match body colour.
- Semi-solid slab single-cutaway body; sunburst or colours.
- Two large black six-polepiece pickups.
- Two controls (volume, tone) and three-way selector, all on inverted metal plate; side-mounted jack socket.
- Small tortoiseshell plastic, or white pearl, tortoiseshell or black laminated plastic pickguard.
- Six-saddle small bridge with through-body stringing.

■ Custom Shop production.

SET NECK TELECASTER *1991-95* Two coverless humbuckers, glued-in neck.
- Mahogany glued-in neck with rosewood fingerboard (pao ferro from 1993); 22 frets; truss-rod adjuster at headstock end; two string-guides; neck and headstock face match body colour.
- Semi-solid slab single-cutaway bound body; various colours.
- Two black coverless humbucker pickups.
- Two controls (volume, tone), three-way selector and coil-tap, all on body; side-mounted jack socket.
- No pickguard.
- Six-saddle small bridge with through-body stringing.

■ Custom Shop production.

SET NECK TELECASTER COUNTRY ARTIST *1992-95* One humbucker and one single-coil, glued-in neck.
Similar to **SET NECK TELECASTER**, except:
- One black coverless humbucker (at neck) and one black six-polepiece pickup (angled in bridgeplate).
- Five-screw tortoiseshell laminated plastic small pickguard.
- Six-saddle flat bridge with through-body stringing.
- Gold-plated hardware.

■ Custom Shop production.

SET NECK TELECASTER FLOYD ROSE *1991-92* Two coverless humbuckers and one single-coil, glued-in neck, locking vibrato system.
Similar to **SET NECK TELECASTER**, except:
- Ebony fingerboard; locking nut.
- Two black coverless humbuckers and one black six-polepiece pickup (in centre).
- Two controls (volume, tone), five-way selector and coil-tap, all on body; side-mounted jack socket.
- Twin-pivot locking bridge/vibrato unit.

■ Custom Shop production.

SET NECK TELECASTER PLUS *1991-92* Two coverless humbuckers, glued-in neck, vibrato.
Similar to **SET NECK TELECASTER**, except:
- Ebony fingerboard; locking tuners; roller nut.
- Twin-pivot bridge/vibrato unit.

■ Custom Shop production.

SPARKLE TELECASTER *1992-95* Coloured sparkle finish on body.
- Fretted maple neck, or maple neck with rosewood fingerboard; truss-rod adjuster at body end; one string-guide.
- Slab single-cutaway body; various sparkle colours.
- One plain metal-cover pickup (at neck) and one black six-polepiece pickup (angled in bridgeplate).
- Two controls (volume, tone) and three-way selector, all on metal plate adjoining pickguard; side-mounted jack socket.
- Eight-screw white laminated plastic pickguard.
- Three-saddle raised-sides bridge with through-body stringing.

■ Custom Shop production.

SPECIAL EDITION 1994 TELECASTER *1994* Commemorative neckplate.
Similar to **AMERICAN STANDARD TELECASTER** (see listing in earlier Regular Telecasters section), except:
- Body black or blond; commemorative neckplate.
- Eight-screw grey pearl or tortoiseshell laminated plastic pickguard.

TELE PLUS first version *1990-95* Three Lace Sensor pickups (two at bridge).
- Fretted maple neck or maple neck with rosewood fingerboard; 22 frets; truss-rod adjuster at headstock end; one string-guide.
- Slab single-cutaway body; sunburst or colours.
- Three black plain-top Lace Sensor pickups (two in single separate surround at bridge).

- Two controls (volume, tone), three-way selector and coil-switch, all on metal plate adjoining pickguard; side-mounted jack socket.
- Eight-screw white laminated plastic pickguard.
- Six-saddle small bridge with through-body stringing.

TELE PLUS second version *1995-98* Three Lace Sensor pickups (one angled in bridgeplate).
- Fretted maple neck or maple neck with rosewood fingerboard; 22 frets; truss-rod adjuster at headstock end; one string-guide.
- Slab single-cutaway bound body; sunburst or colours.
- Three plain-top Lace Sensor pickups (bridgeplate pickup angled).
- Two controls (volume, tone) and three-way selector, all on metal plate adjoining pickguard; side-mounted jack socket.
- Eight-screw white pearl or tortoiseshell laminated plastic pickguard.
- Six-saddle flat bridge with through-body stringing.

TELE PLUS DELUXE *1991-92* Three Lace Sensor pickups (two at bridge), vibrato.
Similar to **TELE PLUS first version**, except:
- No string-guide; locking tuners; roller nut.
- Twin-pivot bridge/vibrato unit.

TELE-SONIC *1998-2004* Model name on headstock
- Maple neck with rosewood fingerboard, 628mm (24 3/4") scale, 22 frets; truss-rod adjuster at headstock end; one string-guide; black-face headstock.
- Semi-solid slab single-cutaway body; sunburst or colours.
- Two metal-surround six-polepiece six-screw pickups.
- Four controls (two volume, two tone) and three-way selector, all on body; side-mounted jack socket.
- Six-screw black laminated plastic pickguard.
- Two-saddle (six-saddle from 2003) wrapover bridge/tailpiece.

TELE SUB-SONIC *2002-current* Model name on headstock, extended-scale neck.
- Fretted maple neck; 686mm (27") scale, 22 frets; truss-rod adjuster at body end; one string-guide; Sub-Sonic on headstock.
- Slab single-cutaway body; sunburst or colours.
- One plain metal-cover pickup with visible height-adjustment screws (at neck) and one black six-polepiece pickup (angled in bridgeplate).
- Two controls (volume, tone) and three-way selector, all on inverted metal plate adjoining pickguard; side-mounted jack socket.
- Eight-screw white laminated plastic pickguard.
- Six-saddle flat bridge with through-body stringing.

■ Custom Shop production.

TELECASTER CUSTOM *1972-81* One humbucker and one single-coil, four controls.
- Fretted maple neck, or maple neck with rosewood fingerboard; "bullet" truss-rod adjuster at headstock end; two string-guides; three-screw neckplate.
- Slab single-cutaway body; sunburst or colours.
- One metal-cover split-polepiece humbucker pickup (at neck) and one black six-polepiece pickup (angled in bridgeplate).
- Four controls (two volume, two tone) and three-way selector, all on pickguard; side-mounted jack socket.
- 16-screw black laminated plastic pickguard.
- Six-saddle raised-sides bridge with through-body stringing.

■ Earliest examples with 15-screw pickguard and/or three-saddle raised-sides bridge.
■ Also **ANTIGUA TELECASTER CUSTOM**, with white/brown shaded body finish and matching-colour laminated plastic pickguard (1977-79).
■ For **CUSTOM TELECASTER** (with bound body) see **TELECASTER** listing in earlier Regular Telecasters section.

TELECASTER DELUXE *1972-81* Two covered humbuckers, normal Tele body.
- Fretted maple neck; "bullet" truss-rod adjuster at headstock end; two string-guides; large Stratocaster-style headstock; three-screw neckplate.
- Contoured single-cutaway body; sunburst or colours.
- Two metal-cover split-polepiece humbucker pickups.
- Four controls (two volume, two tone) and three-way selector, all on pickguard; side-mounted jack socket.
- 16-screw black laminated plastic pickguard.
- Six-saddle small bridge with through-body stringing.

■ Some examples with Stratocaster-type six-pivot bridge/vibrato unit.
■ Also **ANTIGUA TELECASTER DELUXE**, with white/brown shaded body finish and matching-colour laminated plastic pickguard (1977-79).

TELECASTER XII 12-string *1995-98* 12-string headstock with model name.
- Fretted maple neck, or maple neck with rosewood fingerboard; truss-rod adjuster at headstock end; one "bracket" string-guide; six-tuners-per-side headstock.
- Slab single-cutaway body; sunburst or colours.
- One plain metal-cover pickup (at neck) and one black six-polepiece pickup (angled in bridgeplate).
- Two controls (volume, tone) and three-way selector, all on metal plate adjoining pickguard; side-mounted jack socket.

- Five-screw black or white plastic, or white pearl laminated plastic pickguard.
- Twelve-saddle bridge with through-body stringing.

■ Custom Shop production.

THINLINE TELECASTER first version *1968-71* F-hole body, two single-coils.

- Maple neck with maple fingerboard (fretted maple neck, or with rosewood fingerboard from 1969); truss-rod adjuster at body end; one string-guide.
- Semi-solid slab single-cutaway body with f-hole; sunburst or colours.
- One plain metal-cover pickup with visible height-adjustment screws (at neck) and one black six-polepiece pickup (angled in bridgeplate).
- Two controls (volume, tone) and three-way selector, all on pickguard; side-mounted jack socket.
- 12-screw pearl laminated plastic pickguard.
- Three-saddle raised-sides bridge with through-body stringing.

THINLINE TELECASTER second version *1971-79* F-hole body, two humbuckers.
Similar to **THINLINE TELECASTER first version**, except:

- Fretted maple neck only; "bullet" truss-rod adjuster at headstock; three-screw neckplate.
- Two metal-cover split-polepiece humbucker pickups.
- 12-screw black, white or white pearl laminated plastic re-styled pickguard.
- Six-saddle small bridge with through-body stringing.

U.S. FAT TELE *1998-2000* One humbucker and one single-coil, five-way selector.
Similar to **AMERICAN STANDARD TELECASTER** (see listing in earlier Regular Telecasters section), except:

- One metal-cover six-polepiece humbucker (at neck) and one black six-polepiece pickup (angled in bridgeplate).
- Five-way selector.

■ Known as **AMERICAN FAT TELE** (2001-03).

WALNUT ELITE TELECASTER See earlier **ELITE TELECASTER** listing.

WAYLON JENNINGS TRIBUTE TELECASTER *1995-current* Signature on headstock.

- Fretted maple neck; truss-rod adjuster at body end; one string-guide; pearl tuner buttons; Scruggs Peg banjo-style de-tuner for 6th string; "W" inlay at 12th fret and Waylon Jennings signature on headstock.
- Slab single-cutaway bound body; black only with white leather inlay.
- One plain metal-cover pickup with visible height-adjustment screws (at neck) and one black six-polepiece pickup (angled in bridgeplate).
- Two controls (volume, tone) and three-way selector, all on metal plate adjoining pickguard; side-mounted jack socket.
- Eight-screw white laminated plastic pickguard.
- Six-saddle flat bridge with through-body stringing.

■ Custom Shop production.

WILL RAY TELECASTER *1998-2001* Signature on headstock, skull markers.

- Maple neck with rosewood fingerboard, skull markers; 22 frets; truss-rod adjuster at headstock end; one string-guide; locking tuners; Will Ray signature on small Stratocaster-style headstock.
- Slab single-cutaway body; gold foil leaf on various colours.
- Two large rectangular white six-polepiece pickups (bridge pickup angled).
- Three controls (volume, two tone) and three-way selector, all on metal plate adjoining pickguard; side-mounted jack socket.
- Eight-screw white pearl laminated plastic re-styled pickguard.
- Modified three-saddle bridge with through-body stringing; optional Hipshot bending device on second string.

■ Custom Shop production.

50th ANNIVERSARY TELECASTER *1996* Commemorative neckplate.
Similar to **AMERICAN STANDARD TELECASTER** (see listing in earlier Regular Telecasters section), except:

- Fretted maple neck only; commemorative neckplate.
- Body sunburst only.
- Gold-plated hardware.

■ Numbered factory production run in an edition of 1,250.

90s TELE THINLINE *1997-2000* F-hole body, 22 frets.

- Fretted maple neck, or maple neck with rosewood fingerboard; 22 frets; truss-rod adjuster at headstock end; one string-guide.
- Semi-solid slab single-cutaway bound body; sunburst or colours.
- One plain metal-cover pickup with visible height-adjustment screws (at neck) and one black six-polepiece pickup (angled in bridgeplate).
- Two controls (volume, tone) and three-way selector, all on pickguard; side-mounted jack socket.
- 12-screw white pearl or tortoiseshell laminated plastic pickguard.
- Six-saddle flat bridge with through-body stringing.

1998 COLLECTORS EDITION TELECASTER *1998* Commemorative fingerboard inlay and neckplate.
Similar to 50s **TELECASTER** (see listing in earlier Replica Telecasters section), except:

- Fretted maple neck with commemorative inlay at 12th fret; commemorative neckplate.
- Body sunburst only.

- Five-screw white plastic pickguard.
- Gold-plated hardware.

■ Numbered factory production run in an edition of 1,998.

Other US Models

Listed here are various Esquires and Nocasters and the Broadcaster.

BROADCASTER *1950-51* Forerunner of the TELECASTER (see listing in earlier Regular Telecasters section) and very similar, but with Broadcaster model name on headstock. Some late examples have only the Fender logo, and these are known unofficially among collectors as Nocasters.

ESQUIRE *1950-69* Model name on headstock, slab single-cutaway body, one pickup.

- Fretted maple neck (1950-59 and 1969), maple neck with rosewood fingerboard (1959-69), maple fingerboard official option (1967-69); truss-rod adjuster at body end; one string-guide.
- Slab single-cutaway body; originally blond only, later sunburst or colours.
- One black six-polepiece pickup (angled in bridgeplate).
- Two controls (volume, tone) and three-way selector, all on metal plate adjoining pickguard; side-mounted jack socket.
- Five-screw (eight-screw from 1959) black plastic pickguard (white plastic from 1954; white laminated plastic from 1963).
- Three-saddle bridge with through-body stringing (strings anchored at bridgeplate not through body 1958-60).

■ Very few earliest 'pre-production' examples without truss-rod, and some have second pickup at neck.

■ Also CUSTOM ESQUIRE, with bound body (1959-69).

NOCASTER See earlier listing for **BROADCASTER** model.

RELIC NOCASTER *1995-98* Distressed-finish replica of 1950-period original with no model name on headstock (see earlier BROADCASTER listing). Custom Shop production.

'51 NOCASTER *1999-current* Replica of 1950-period original with no model name on headstock (see earlier BROADCASTER listing). Available in N.O.S, Closet Classic and Relic versions. Custom Shop production.

'59 ESQUIRE *2003-current* Replica of 1959-period original (see earlier ESQUIRE listing). No through-body stringing. Available in N.O.S, Closet Classic and Relic versions. Custom Shop production.

SEYMOUR DUNCAN SIGNATURE ESQUIRE *2003-current* Signature on headstock.

- Fretted maple neck; truss-rod adjuster at body end; one string-guide; Seymour Duncan signature on headstock.
- Slab single-cutaway body; sunburst only. • One black six-polepiece pickup (angled in bridgeplate).
- Two controls (volume, tone) and three-way selector, all on metal plate adjoining pickguard; side-mounted jack socket.
- Five-screw white plastic pickguard.
- Three-saddle bridge with through-body stringing.

■ Custom Shop production.

Custom Shop

The Fender Custom Shop was officially established in 1987. It now produces three broad types of instruments: one-offs or 'Master Builder' guitars; numbered limited-edition guitars; and catalogued general-production instruments. Guitars in the latter category are noted here in the main US listing, indicated as "Custom Shop production". The one-offs and limited editions are beyond the scope of this reference section. All official Custom Shop instruments carry an appropriate identifying logo on the back of the headstock.

MEXICAN-MADE TELECASTERS

Mexican Telecasters are all listed here in one section.

CONTEMPORARY TELECASTER See later TELE SPECIAL listing.

DELUXE NASHVILLE TELE *1997-current* White six-polepiece pickup in centre position.

Similar to STANDARD TELECASTER (see later listing), except:

- Fretted maple neck, or maple neck with rosewood fingerboard.
- Body sunburst or colours.
- One plain metal-cover pickup with visible height-adjustment screws (at neck), one white six-polepiece pickup (in centre) and one black six-polepiece pickup (angled in bridgeplate).
- White six-polepiece pickup (in centre).
- Two controls (volume, tone) and five-way selector, all on metal plate adjoining pickguard.
- Eight-screw tortoiseshell laminated plastic pickguard.
- Six-saddle raised-sides bridge with through-body stringing.

DELUXE NASHVILLE POWER TELE *1999-current* White six-polepiece pickup in centre position, one dual-concentric control.

Similar to DELUXE NASHVILLE TELE (see earlier listing), except:

- One dual-concentric control (volume, tone for magnetic pickups), one control (volume for piezo pickups) and five-way selector.
- Eight-screw tortoiseshell laminated plastic pickguard.

- Fishman Power Bridge with six piezo-pickup saddles.

JAMES BURTON STANDARD TELECASTER *1995-current* Signature on headstock.
Similar to STANDARD TELECASTER (see later listing), except:
- James Burton signature on headstock.
- Eight-screw white plastic pickguard.
- Six-saddle raised-sides bridge with through-body stringing.

JOHN 5 TELECASTER *2005-current* Headstock with three tuners each side, humbucker at bridge.
- Maple neck with rosewood fingerboard; 22 frets; truss-rod adjuster at headstock end; no string-guide; three tuners each side.
- Slab single-cutaway bound body; black only.
- One plain metal-cover pickup with visible height adjustment screws (at neck) and one black coverless humbucker (in bridgeplate).
- Two controls (volume, tone) on metal plate adjoining pickguard, three-way selector on body ; side-mounted jack socket.
- Eight-screw chromed pickguard.
- Six-saddle flat bridge with through-body stringing.

MUDDY WATERS TELECASTER *2001-current* Amplifier-type black plastic control knobs.
- Maple neck with rosewood fingerboard; truss-rod adjuster at body end; one string-guide; Custom Telecaster on headstock.
- Slab single-cutaway body; red only.
- One plain metal-cover pickup (at neck) and one black six-polepiece pickup (angled in bridgeplate).
- Two controls (volume, tone) and three-way selector, all on metal plate adjoining pickguard; side-mounted jack socket.
- Nine-screw white plastic pickguard.
- Three-saddle raised-sides bridge with through-body stringing.
- Amp-type black plastic control knobs.

SPECIAL TELECASTER See later STANDARD TELECASTER listing.

SQUIER SERIES STANDARD TELECASTER See later TRADITIONAL TELECASTER listing.

STANDARD TELECASTER *1991-current* Modern-style "thick" Fender headstock logo in silver, two single-coils.
- Fretted maple neck; truss-rod adjuster at headstock end; one string-guide.
- Slab single-cutaway body; sunburst or colours.
- One plain metal-cover pickup with visible height-adjustment screws (at neck) and one black six-polepiece pickup (angled in bridgeplate).
- Two controls (volume, tone) and three-way selector, all on metal plate adjoining pickguard; side-mounted jack socket.
- Eight-screw white laminated plastic pickguard.
- Six-saddle flat bridge/tailpiece (no through-body stringing).

■ Originally known as SPECIAL TELECASTER in UK.

TELE SPECIAL *1994-96* Humbucker at neck, black pickguard.
Similar to STANDARD TELECASTER (see previous listing), except:
- One metal-cover six-polepiece humbucker (at neck) and one black six-polepiece pickup (angled in bridgeplate).
- Two controls (volume, tone) and five-way selector.
- Eight-screw black laminated plastic pickguard.
- Six-saddle raised-sides bridge with through-body stringing.

■ Known as CONTEMPORARY TELECASTER in UK.

TEX-MEX TELE SPECIAL *1997* Humbucker at neck, white pickguard.
Similar to STANDARD TELECASTER (see earlier listing), except:
- One metal-cover six-polepiece humbucker (at neck) and one black six-polepiece pickup (angled in bridgeplate).
- Two controls (volume, tone) and five-way selector.
- Six-saddle raised-sides bridge with through-body stringing.

TRADITIONAL TELECASTER *1996-97* Modern-style "thick" Fender headstock logo in black, two single-coils.
Similar to vintage-style Telecaster, except:
- Fretted maple neck; truss-rod adjuster at headstock end; one string-guide.
- Slab single-cutaway body; various colours.
- One plain metal-cover pickup with visible height-adjustment screws (at neck) and one black six-polepiece pickup (angled in bridgeplate).
- Two controls (volume, tone) and three-way selector, all on metal plate adjoining pickguard; side-mounted jack socket.
- Eight-screw white laminated plastic pickguard.
- Six-saddle flat bridge/tailpiece (no through-body stringing).

■ Previously known as SQUIER SERIES STANDARD TELECASTER, with small Squier Series logo on headstock (1994-96).

50s TELECASTER *1998-current* Replica of 1952-period US original (see TELECASTER listing in earlier US-made Regular Telecasters section).

60s TELECASTER *2002-current* Replica of 1960-period US original (see TELECASTER listing in earlier US-made Regular Telecasters section).

'69 TELECASTER THINLINE *1998-current* Replica of 1969-period US original with two single-coils (see **THINLINE TELECASTER first version** listing in earlier US-made Revised Telecasters section).

'72 TELECASTER CUSTOM *1999-current* Replica of 1972-period US original with humbucker and single-coil (see **TELECASTER CUSTOM** listing in earlier US-made Revised Telecasters section).

'72 TELECASTER DELUXE *2004-current* Replica of 1972-period US original with two humbuckers (see **TELECASTER DELUXE** listing in earlier US-made Revised Telecasters section).

'72 TELECASTER THINLINE *1999-current* Replica of 1972-period US original with two humbuckers (see **THINLINE TELECASTER second version** listing in earlier US-made Revised Telecasters section).

50s ESQUIRE *2005-current* Replica of 1950-period US original (see earlier **ESQUIRE** listing).

JAPANESE-MADE TELECASTERS

Japanese Telecasters are divided into three sections: REPLICA; REVISED; OTHER.

Replica Telecasters

Listed in alphabetical order here are the Japan-made models for sale outside Japan that replicate various standard US-made Telecasters (see earlier US-made Regular Telecasters and US-made Revised Telecasters sections).

BLUE FLOWER TELECASTER *1986-current* Replica of 1969-period US original with blue floral pattern-finish body (see **TELECASTER** listing in earlier US-made Regular Telecasters section).

CUSTOM TELECASTER '62 *1985-current* Replica of 1962-period US original with bound-body (see **TELECASTER** listing in earlier US-made Regular Telecasters section). Foto Flame fake figured wood finish option (1994-96).

PAISLEY TELECASTER *1986-current* Replica of 1969-period US original with paisley-pattern body finish (see **TELECASTER** listing in earlier US-made Regular Telecasters section).

ROSEWOOD TELECASTER *1986-current* Replica of 1969-period US original with rosewood neck and body (see **TELECASTER** listing in earlier US-made Regular Telecasters section).

TELECASTER CUSTOM '72 *1986-98* Replica of 1972-period US original with humbucker and single-coil (see **TELECASTER CUSTOM** listing in earlier US-made Revised Telecasters section).

THINLINE TELECASTER '69 *1986-98* Replica of 1969-period US original with two single-coils (see **THINLINE TELECASTER first version** listing in earlier US-made Revised Telecasters section).

THINLINE TELECASTER '72 *1986-98* Replica of 1972-period US original with two humbuckers (see **THINLINE TELECASTER second version** listing in earlier US-made Revised Telecasters section).

50s TELECASTER *1990-98* Replica of 1952-period US original (see **TELECASTER** listing in earlier US-made Regular Telecasters section). Previously known in UK as **SQUIER SERIES '52 TELECASTER**, with small Squier Series logo on headstock (1982-83). Sold under the actual Squier brandname (1983-85) and new Fender version introduced in 1990, although Japanese market manufacture continuous since 1982. Foto Flame fake figured wood finish option (1994).

60s TELECASTER *1994* Replica of 1960s-period Telecaster (see **TELECASTER** listing in earlier US-made Regular Telecasters section) but with Foto Flame fake figured wood finish neck and body in natural only. Replaced by **FOTO FLAME TELE** (see later listing in Japan-made Revised Telecasters section).

Revised Telecasters

Listed here are the models we regard as different to the standard Regular Telecasters (see earlier US-made Regular Stratocasters section).

AERODYNE TELE *2004-current* Model name on headstock.
- Maple neck with rosewood fingerboard; 22 frets; truss-rod adjuster at headstock end; one string guide; black headstock face; Aerodyne Series on headstock.
- Single-cutaway bound body with carved top; black only.
- One large black rectangular six-polepiece pickup (at neck) and one black six-polepiece pickup (angled in bridgeplate).
- Two controls (volume, tone) and three-way selector, all on body; side-mounted jack socket.
- No pickguard.
- Six-saddle flat bridge with through-body stringing.

BUCK OWENS TELECASTER *1998* Signature on headstock, red, silver and blue sparkle striped body front.
- Maple neck with rosewood fingerboard; truss-rod adjuster at body end; one string- guide; red, silver and blue sparkle striped headstock face; Buck Owens signature on headstock.
- Slab single-cutaway bound body;

red, silver and blue sparkle striped finish to front.

- One plain metal-cover pickup (at neck) and one black six-polepiece pickup (angled in bridgeplate).
- Two controls (volume, tone) and three-way selector, all on metal plate adjoining pickguard; side-mounted jack socket.
- Eight-screw gold pickguard.
- Three-saddle raised-sides bridge with through-body stringing.
- Gold-plated hardware.

CONTEMPORARY TELECASTER first version *1985-87* Black neck, two humbuckers.

- Maple neck with rosewood fingerboard; 22 frets; truss-rod adjuster at headstock end; string clamp; black neck.
- Slab single-cut body; various colours.
- Two black coverless humbuckers.
- Two controls (volume, tone), three-way selector and coil-switch, all on body; side-mounted jack socket.
- No pickguard.
- Two -pivot bridge/vibrato unit.
- Black-plated hardware.

CONTEMPORARY TELECASTER second version *1985-87* Black neck, two single-coils and one humbucker.
Similar to **CONTEMPORARY TELECASTER first version**, except:

- Two black six-polepiece pickups and one black coverless humbucker (at bridge).
- Two controls (volume, tone) and three mini-switches, all on body.

FOTO FLAME TELECASTER *1995-96* Fake figured wood finish on neck and body, two single-coils.
Similar to **60s TELECASTER** (see earlier listing in Replica Telecasters section), except:

- Foto Flame fake figured wood finish body; sunbursts or natural.
- Eight-screw white or white pearl laminated plastic pickguard.

FRANCIS ROSSI SIGNATURE TELECASTER *2004-05* Signature on headstock.

- Fretted maple neck; 21 frets; truss-rod adjuster at body end; one string-guide; Francis Rossi signature on headstock.
- Slab single-cutaway body with circular hole; satin black with green front only.
- Three white plain-top pickups (bridge pickup angled in cut-down bridgeplate).
- Two controls (volume, tone) and five-way selector, all on metal plate adjoining pickguard; side-mounted jack socket.
- Eight-screw white plastic laminate pickguard.
- Six-saddle small bridge with through-body stringing.

HMT ACOUSTIC-ELECTRIC first version *1991-94* Stratocaster-style headstock, wooden-base bridge.

- Maple neck with rosewood fingerboard; 638mm (25.1=) scale, 22 frets; truss-rod adjuster at headstock end; one string-guide; large Stratocaster-style headstock with black-face.
- Enlarged semi-solid slab single-cutaway bound body with f-hole; sunburst or colours.
- One black plain-top Lace Sensor (angled at neck) and piezo pickup (in bridge).
- Three controls (volume, tone, pan,) all on body; side-mounted jack socket; active circuit.
- No pickguard.
- Single-saddle wooden-base bridge.

HMT ACOUSTIC-ELECTRIC second version *1995-97* Telecaster headstock, wooden-base bridge.
Similar to **HMT ACOUSTIC-ELECTRIC first version** (see previous entry), except:

- Telecaster headstock.
- Body sunburst or black.
- One black plain-top pickup (angled at neck) and piezo pickup (in bridge).

HMT TELECASTER first version *1991-92* Stratocaster-style headstock, F-hole body, two humbuckers.

- Maple neck with rosewood fingerboard; 638mm (25.1=) scale, 22 frets; truss-rod adjuster at headstock end; Stratocaster-style black-face headstock.
- Larger semi-solid slab single-cutaway bound body with f-hole; sunburst or colours.
- Two black coverless humbuckers.
- Two controls (volume, tone), three-way selector and coil-switch, all on body; side-mounted jack socket.
- No pickguard.
- Six-saddle small bridge with through-body stringing.

HMT TELECASTER second version *1991-92* Drooped headstock with long "streamlined" Fender logo, f-hole body, angled Lace Sensor and humbucker.
Similar to **HMT TELECASTER first version**, except:

- Split-triangle markers; locking nut; long "streamlined" Fender logo on drooped black-face headstock.
- One black plain-top Lace Sensor pickup (angled at neck) and one black coverless humbucker (at bridge).
- Two -pivot locking bridge/vibrato unit.

JD TELECASTER *1992-99* "JD" on headstock, black six-polepiece pickup at neck.

- Fretted maple neck; truss-rod adjuster at body end; one string-guide; Jerry Donahue initials on headstock.
- Slab single-cutaway bound body; sunburst or colours.
- Two black six-polepiece pickups (bridgeplate pickup angled).
- Two controls (volume, tone) and five-way selector, all on metal plate

adjoining pickguard; side-mounted jack socket.
- Eight-screw black laminated plastic pickguard.
- Three-saddle raised-sides bridge with through-body stringing.

■ Based on signature model of US Custom Shop.

NOKIE EDWARDS TELECASTER
1996-97 Signature on headstock, two twin-blade humbuckers.
- Maple neck with ebony fingerboard; 22 frets; truss-rod adjuster at body end; brass nut; optional Scruggs Peg banjo-style de-tuner for 6th string; Nokie Edwards signature on headstock.
- Single-cutaway body with figured front; natural only.
- Two black twin-blade humbucker pickups.
- Two controls (volume, tone) and three-way selector, all on body, side-mounted jack socket.
- No pickguard.
- Six-saddle small bridge with through-body stringing.
- Gold-plated hardware.

■ Optional Nokie Edwards body logo.

RICK PARFITT SIGNATURE TELECASTER *2004-05* Signature on headstock.
- Maple neck with rosewood fingerboard: 21 frets; truss-rod adjuster at body end; one string-guide' Rick Parfitt signature on headstock.
- Slab single-cutaway body; satin white only.
- One plain metal-cover pickup (at neck) and one black six-polepiece pickup (angled in cut down bridgeplate).
- Two controls (volume, tone) and three-way selector, all on metal plate adjoining pickguard; side-mounted jack socket.
- Eight-screw black plastic pickguard.
- Four-saddle wrapover bridge/tailpiece with through-body stringing.
- Some hardware gold-plated.

SPECIAL TELECASTER
UK designation for **STANDARD TELECASTER** (see later listing).

SQUIER SERIES '52 TELECASTER
See earlier **50s TELECASTER** listing in Replica Telecasters section.

STANDARD TELECASTER *1988-91*
Two string-guides, five-screw pickguard, six-saddle bridge/tailpiece with no through-body stringing.
- Fretted maple neck; truss-rod adjuster at body end; two string-guides.
- Slab single-cutaway body; black or blond.
- One plain metal cover pickup (at neck) and one black six-polepiece pickup (angled in bridgeplate).
- Two controls (volume, tone) and three-way selector, all on metal plate adjoining pickguard; side-mounted jack socket.
- Five-screw white plastic pickguard.
- Six-saddle flat bridge/tailpiece with no through-body stringing.

■ Previously marketed under the Squier brandname (1985-88). Production moved to Mexico from 1991 (see **STANDARD STRATOCASTER** listing in earlier Mexico-made Stratocasters section). Known as **SPECIAL TELECASTER** in UK.

WILL RAY JAZZ-A-CASTER *1997-98*
Signature and model name on headstock, two large white pickups.
- Maple neck with rosewood fingerboard, triangle markers; 22 frets; truss-rod adjuster at headstock end; one string guide; locking tuners; "Hellecasters" inlay at 12th fret; Will Ray signature on small Stratocaster-style headstock.
- Slab single-cutaway body; gold foil leaf only.
- Two large white rectangular six-polepiece pickups (bridge pickup angled).
- Two controls (volume, tone) and four-way selector, all on metal plate adjoining pickguard; side-mounted jack socket.
- Eight-screw white pearl laminated plastic pickguard.
- Modified six-saddle bridge with through-body stringing; Hipshot bending device on 2nd string.

50s TELECASTER WITH BIGSBY
2005-current Fretted maple neck, Bigsby vibrato tailpiece
- Fretted maple neck; truss-rod adjuster at body end.
- Slab single-cutaway body; blond or white.
- One plain metal-cover pickup (at neck) and one black six-polepiece pickup (angled in bridgeplate).
- Two controls (volume, tone) and three-way selector, all on metal plate adjoining pickguard; side-mounted jack socket.
- White laminated plastic pickguard.
- Six-saddle bridge, separate Bigsby vibrato tailpiece.

60s TELECASTER WITH BIGSBY
2005-current Bound body, rosewood fingerboard, Bigsby vibrato tailpiece.
- Maple neck with rosewood fingerboard; truss-rod adjuster at body end; one string-guide.
- Slab single-cutaway bound body; sunburst or red.
- One plain metal-cover pickup (at neck) and one black six-polepiece pickup (angled in bridgeplate).
- Two controls (volume, tone) and three-way selector, all on metal plate adjoining pickguard; side-mounted jack socket.
- Eight-screw white laminated plastic pickguard.
- Six-saddle bridge, separate Bigsby vibrato tailpiece.

90s TELECASTER CUSTOM *1995-97* Black or white bound body with matching headstock face, pearl pickguard, gold-plated hardware.

- Maple neck with rosewood fingerboard; truss-rod adjuster at body end; one string-guide; black- or white-face headstock.
- Slab single-cutaway bound body; black or white.
- One plain metal-cover pickup (at neck) and one black six-polepiece pickup (angled in bridgeplate).
- Two controls (volume, tone) and three-way selector, all on metal plate adjoining pickguard; side-mounted jack socket.
- Eight-screw grey or white pearl laminated plastic pickguard.
- Six-saddle flat bridge with through-body stringing.
- Gold-plated hardware.

90s TELECASTER DELUXE *1995-97* Contoured body, three six-polepiece pickups, inverted control plate.

- Maple neck with rosewood fingerboard; truss-rod adjuster at body end; one string-guide.
- Single-cut body; sunburst or colours.
- Two white six-polepiece pickups (neck and centre) and one black six-polepiece pickup (angled in bridgeplate).
- Two controls (volume, tone) and five-way selector, all on inverted metal plate adjoining pickguard; side-mounted jack socket.
- Eight-screw white pearl laminated plastic pickguard.
- Six-saddle flat bridge with through-body stringing.

■ Foto Flame fake figured wood finish option (1995-96).

Other Japanese Models

A couple of Esquires.

CUSTOM ESQUIRE *1986-93* Replica of 1962-period US original with bound body (see **ESQUIRE** listing in earlier Other US-made Models section).

ESQUIRE *1986-93* Replica of 1954-period US original (see **ESQUIRE** listing in earlier Other US-made Models section).

KOREAN-MADE TELECASTERS

Many models made in Korea for Fender bear the Squier brandname and so are beyond the scope of this reference section. However, some have prominently featured the Fender logo, and these are listed here. All have 'Made in Korea' somewhere on the instrument.

BLACKOUT TELECASTER *2004-current* All-black finish, no front markers.

- Glued-in maple neck with rosewood fingerboard, no front markers; 22 frets; truss-rod adjuster at headstock end; two string-guides.
- Single-cutaway body; black only.
- Two black coverless humbuckers. • Two controls (volume, tone) and three-way selector, all on body; side-mounted jack socket.
- No pickguard.
- Six-saddle small bridge with through-body stringing.
- Black-plated hardware.

ESQUIRE CUSTOM CELTIC *2003* Celtic inlay at 12th fret.

- Glued-in maple neck with rosewood fingerboard, no front markers; 22 frets; truss-rod adjuster at headstock end; two string-guides; Celtic inlay at 12th fret.
- Single-cutaway body with carved top; satin silver only.
- One black coverless humbucker (at bridge).
- One control (volume) on body; side-mounted jack socket.
- No pickguard.
- Six-saddle small bridge with through-body stringing.
- Black-plated hardware.

ESQUIRE CUSTOM GT *2003* Single humbucker, white centre stripe.

- Glued-in maple neck with rosewood fingerboard; 22 frets; truss-rod adjuster at headstock end; two string-guides. • Single-cutaway body with carved top; various colours with white centre stripe.
- One black coverless humbucker (at bridge).
- One control (volume) on body; side-mounted jack socket.
- No pickguard.
- Six-saddle small bridge with through-body stringing.
- Black-plated hardware.

ESQUIRE CUSTOM SCORPION *2003* Scorpion inlay at 12th fret.

- Glued-in maple neck with bound rosewood fingerboard, no front markers; 22 frets; truss-rod adjuster at headstock end; two string-guides. • Single-cutaway bound body with carved top; black only.
- One black coverless humbucker (at bridge).
- One control (volume) on body; side-mounted jack socket.
- No pickguard.
- Six-saddle small bridge with through-body stringing.
- Black-plated hardware.

LITE ASH TELECASTER *2004-current* Figured maple neck with figured maple fingerboard, two string guides.

- Figured maple neck with figured maple fingerboard; 22 frets; truss-rod adjuster at headstock end; two string-guides.
- Slab single-cutaway body; natural or colours.
- One plain metal-cover pickup (at neck) and one black six-polepiece pickup (angled in bridgeplate).
- Two controls (volume, tone) and

three-way selector, all on metal plate adjoining pickguard; side-mounted jack socket.
- Eight-screw black plastic pickguard.
- Three-saddle raised-sides bridge (no through-body stringing).

SQUIER SERIES STANDARD TELECASTER *1992-94* Small Squier Series logo on headstock.
- Fretted maple neck; 21 frets; truss-rod adjuster at headstock end; one string-guide; small Squier Series logo on headstock.
- Slab single-cutaway body; various colours.
- One plain metal-cover pickup with visible height-adjustment screws (at neck) and one black six-polepiece pickup (angled in bridgeplate).
- Two controls (volume, tone) and three-way selector, all on metal plate adjoining pickguard; side-mounted jack socket.
- Eight-screw white plastic pickguard.
- Six-saddle flat bridge/tailpiece (no through-body stringing).

■ Replaced by Mexican-made version in 1994 (see **TRADITIONAL TELECASTER** in earlier Mexican-made Telecasters section).

TELECASTER CUSTOM FMT *2003-current* Glued-in neck, bound body with figured, carved top.
- Glued-in maple neck with bound rosewood fingerboard; 22 frets; truss-rod adjuster at headstock end; two string-guides. • Single-cutaway bound body with figured carved top; various colours.
- Two black coverless humbuckers. • Two controls (volume, tone) and three-way selector, all on body; side-mounted jack socket.
- No pickguard.
- Six-saddle small bridge with through-body stringing.
- Smoked chrome or black-plated hardware.

SQUIER

Japanese-made Fender instruments exported into Europe in the early 1980s – and later elsewhere – were issued with a brandname that had been borrowed from the US Fender-owned V.C. Squier string company.

Fender's policy was that the Squier line should cater for lower-price instruments. The intention was that this would maintain the company's ever-expanding coverage of the guitar market – but not by cheapening the prime Fender name itself.

The Squier logo, supported by a small but important line reading 'by Fender', appeared on an increasing number of models during the decade.

At first these models came from Japan, but escalating production costs meant a move to cheaper sources of manufacturing.

Korea came on line in 1985, and India made a brief contribution in the late 1980s for early Squier II examples (or Sunn, another borrowed name).

Fender's facility in Mexico helped out too in the early 1990s, and more recently China and Indonesia have entered the picture, providing entry-level electrics with the kudos of a Fender connection.

Periodic returns to Japanese production have yielded impressive results, such as the Silver and Vista series, while the Pro Tone line and more recent efforts offer evidence of improving Korean quality.

The continuing success story of Squier makes this a very important support brand for Fender, often exhibiting a level of design and build quality that ably exceeds its apparent status as a second-string line.

Dating Telecasters

Finding a method to date a guitar is important. Not only can it help satisfy our natural curiosity about the origins of an instrument but, in the case of desirable instruments, the vintage can have a great bearing on the guitar's value. The Fender brand has its fair share of collectables, of course, and as prices of the more sought-after models often reach very high levels, any corroboratory clues that indicate the year of production will take on increased importance.

Changes specific to each Fender model have been indicated in the main instrument listings here. Although the respective features for some individual models can provide more dating clues than for others, there are comparatively few aspects that are consistent across all the Fender models – and fewer still that have chronological significance. We've brought together on the following page some of the few relevant general pointers to the period of production of US-made models, but even these should not be regarded as infallible.

Neckplate

The standard method used by Fender to fix a guitar neck to the body is with four screws (often erroneously called 'bolts' in Fenderspeak). This is normally accomplished using a metal neckplate to reinforce the joint.

The rectangular four-screw neckplate has been used since the inception of the first Fender solidbody electric in order to provide a simple and secure foundation for the neck.

From 1971 to 1981 a restyled, three-screw version (actually two screws and one bolt) was used on three Telecasters – Custom, Deluxe, and Thinline – as well as the Stratocaster and Starcaster, After 1981, Fender reverted to the four-screw type for most instruments (excluding any set-neck models, of course).

From 1954 to 1976 the neckplate carried a stamped serial number. From 1976 onwards the serial appears on the headstock face, except for the Vintage reissues and limited editions.

From 1965 to 1983 the neckplate (both four- and three-screw types) was stamped with a large, reversed 'F'.

Tuners

It was not easy at first for Fender to find machine heads (tuners) to suit Leo's ideal of a small, neat headstock with straight string-pull.

The problem was solved by using products supplied by the Chicago-based Kluson company, although even these had to be cut down by Race & Olmsted to squeeze them into the minimal length available.

The Klusons used by Fender each had a 'safety string post', a slotted shaft with a central vertical hole designed to take the end of the string and thus eliminate the unsightly and dangerous protruding string length. These tuners were used from 1950 to 1966, and the following variations of the markings on their metal covers can provide an indication of date.

Version 1, used in 1950 and 1951, has "Kluson Deluxe" and "Pat. Appld" stamped on the cover.

Version 2, used from 1951 to 1957, has no markings on the cover.

Version 3, used from 1957 to 1964, has "Kluson Deluxe" stamped in a single, central, vertical line on the cover.

Version 4, used from 1964 to 1966, has "Kluson" and "Deluxe" stamped in two parallel, vertical lines on the cover.

Due to supply and quality problems with Kluson, Fender wanted a tuner produced in-house, and in 1965 contracted Race & Olmsted to supply a revised, cheaper design. The result was a tuner with an angled baseplate, 'F'-stamped cover, and a less rounded button. It was used on Fender instruments until 1976 when it was replaced by a more competitively-priced version made by the German Schaller company, until 1983. Although ostensibly very similar in appearance, the Schaller unit has a different construction, and can be distinguished by its closed cover, with no visible axle-end on the side.

Neck/Fingerboard Construction

From 1950 to 1959 Fender used a fretted one-piece maple neck, with no separate fingerboard.

From 1959 to 1962 the top of the maple neck was planed flat and fitted with a rosewood fingerboard, flat on the base and cambered on top. The appearance of the straight join between fingerboard and neck when viewed from the body end of the neck has led to its description as a "slab board".

From 1962 to 1983 the top of the maple neck itself was cambered and then fitted with a thin-section rosewood fingerboard that followed the same curve. Again, the appearance of the curved join of the neck-end is the reason for its 'veneer' description. A maple fingerboard was offered as an option, officially from 1967 but often supplied prior to that date. In 1969 the fretted one-piece maple neck was reinstated as an alternative to the rosewood fingerboard.

Since 1983 Fender has reverted to a 'slab' rosewood fingerboard option, while the all-maple equivalent is still the principal version.

Neck Dates

During production, Fender dates various components, and one of the most consistent and obvious is the neck. The date is to be found on the body-end, either pencilled or rubber-stamped. There have been times when the neck did not carry this useful information, the longest period being between 1973 and 1981, and for these guitars other dating clues must suffice.

SERIAL NUMBERS

These should be regarded merely as a guide to dating, and the production year of a guitar should ideally be confirmed by other age-related aspects. As is usual with a mass-manufacturer, Fender does not assign serial numbers in exact chronological order, and number-bearing components such as neckplates have rarely been used in strict rotation. As a result, apparent discrepancies and contradictions of as much as several years can and do occur. Depending on the production period, serial numbers are located either on the guitar's bridgeplate, backplate, neckplate, or on the front or back of the headstock.

US and Mexico numbers

These numbers represent the bulk of Fender's US and Mexican production, although the late-1990s California models usually feature AMXN serial prefixes, reflecting their mix of

US number series	Approx. year(s)
Up to 6,000	1950-54
Up to 10,000 (4 or 5 digits, inc 0 or - prefix)	1954-56
10,000s (4 or 5 digits, inc 0 or - prefix)	1955-56
10,000s to 20,000s (5 or 6 digits, inc 0 or - prefix)	1957
20,000s to 30,000s (5 or 6 digits, inc 0 or - prefix)	1958
30,000s to 40,000s	1959
40,000s to 50,000s	1960
50,000s to 70,000s	1961
60,000s to 90,000s	1962
80,000s to 90,000s	1963
Up to L10,000 (L + 5 digits)	1963
L10,000s to L20,000s (L + 5 digits)	1963
L20,000s to L50,000s (L + 5 digits)	1964
L50,000s to L90,000s (L + 5 digits)	1965
100,000s	1965
100,000s to 200,000s	1966-67
200,000s	1968
200,000s to 300,000s	1969-70
300,000s	1971-72
300,000s to 500,000s	1973
400,000s to 500,000s	1974-75
500,000s to 700,000s	1976
800,000s to 900,000s	1979-81
76 or S6 + 5 digits	1976
S7 or S8 + 5 digits	1977
S7, S8 or S9 + 5 digits	1978
S9 or E0 + 5 digits	1979
S9, E0 or E1 + 5 digits	1980-81
E1, E2 or E3 + 5 digits	1982
E2 or E3 + 5 digits	1983
E3 or E4 + 5 digits	1984-87
E4 + 5 digits	1987
E4 or E8 + 5 digits	1988
E8 or E9 + 5 digits	1989-90
E9 or N9 + 5 digits	1990-91
N0 + 5 digits	1990-91
N1 + 5/6 digits	1991-92
N2 + 5/6 digits	1992-93
N3 + 5/6 digits	1993-94
N4 + 5/6 digits	1994-95
N5 + 5/6 digits	1995-96
N6 + 5/6 digits	1996-97
N7 + 5/6 digits	1997-98
N8 + 5/6 digits	1998-99
N9 + 5/6 digits	1999-2000
Z0 + 5/6 digits	2000-01
Z1 + 5/6 digits	2001-02
Z2 + 5/6 digits	2002-03
Z3 + 5/6 digits	2003-04
Z4 + 5/6 digits	2004-05

Japan number series	Approx. year(s)
JV + 5 digits	1982-84
SQ + 5 digits	1983-84
E + 6 digits	1984-87
A + 6 digits	1985-86, 1997-98
B + 6 digits	1985-86, 1998-99
C + 6 digits	1985-86
F + 6 digits	1986-87
G + 6 digits	1987-88
H + 6 digits	1988-89
I + 6 digits	1989-90
J + 6 digits	1989-90
K + 6 digits	1990-91
L + 6 digits	1991-92
M + 6 digits	1992-93
N + 6 digits	1993-94
O + 6 digits	1993-94
P + 6 digits	1993-94
Q + 6 digits	1993-94
S + 6 digits	1994-95
T + 6 digits	1994-95
U + 6 digits	1995-96
V + 6 digits	1996-97
N + 5 digits	1995-96
O + 5 digits	1997-2000
P + 5 digits	1999-2002
Q + 5 digits	2002-04
R + 5 digits	2004-05

Mexico number series	Approx. year(s)
MN1 + 5/6 digits	1991-92
MN2 + 5/6 digits	1992-93
MN3 + 5/6 digits	1993-94
MN4 + 5/6 digits	1994-95
MN5 + 5/6 digits	1995-96
MN6 + 5/6 digits	1996-97
MN7 + 5/6 digits	1997-98
MN8 + 5/6 digits	1998-99
MN9 + 5/6 digits	1999-2000
MZ0 + 5/6 digits	2001-02
MZ2 + 5/6 digits	2002-03
MZ3 + 5/6 digits	2003-04
MZ4 + 5/6 digits	2004-05

American and Mexican manufacture. There have been and continue to be various anomalies, odd series, special prefixes and the like, but these have no overall dating relevance and are not listed. Also excluded are the series used on Vintage replica reissues, limited editions, signature instruments and so on, as these are specific to certain models and not directly pertinent to production year.

The listings here do not apply to Fenders which originate from countries other than the USA and Mexico; these (and Squier-brand instruments) have their own various number series, which unfortunately do sometimes duplicate those in the US system; prefixes include YN for China and CN for Korea (meaning the Cort factory). Any confusion has to be resolved by studying other aspects of the instruments to determine correct origins (often simply determined by a "Made In..." stamp) and production dates.

Japan numbers

Fender Japan production commenced in 1982 and the company has used a series of prefixes to indicate the year of manufacture. However, the data shown here is approximate and again should be used as a general guide only.

Fender Japan has confirmed evidence that certain series have been used beyond the production spans listed above, in particular the A-, C- and G-prefix numbers. Also, note the reversion to N, O, P, Q, R etc prefixes for more recent production, which will almost certainly cause confusion in the future. Once again these facts underline the need for caution when dating a Fender – and indeed most other guitars – by using only serial numbers.

Part numbers

Since the 1970s many Fender catalogues and pricelists have employed 'part' numbers to make the process of ordering and stock-keeping easier for distributors and dealers. Each version and variation of a guitar is allocated a specific number so that, for instance, a 2005 sunburst Fender American Telecaster model might have the number 010-8400-700. The digits provide various pieces of information about the model type, fingerboard wood, hardware options, finish colour, and even if a case is included in the price. But the second and third digits (10 in our example) are particularly useful as they can indicate the instrument's country of origin. To the best of our knowledge – and this information is not supplied by Fender – the codes have indicated the following sources.

10 US (Fender)
11 US (Fender)
13 Mexico/US (Fender, Squier); formerly Japan (Fender)
14 US/Mexico (Fender)
15 US Custom Shop (Fender)
25 Japan (Fender)
26 Korea (Fender); formerly Japan (Squier)
27 Japan (Fender, Squier); formerly Korea (Squier)
28 China (Squier); formerly Japan (Fender), India (Squier II, Sunn)
29 India (Squier II, Sunn)
31 China (Squier); formerly Japan (Heartfield)
32 Indonesia or Korea or China (Squier); formerly Japan (Squier)
33 Korea (Fender, Squier) or China (Squier); formerly India (Squier II)
34 Korea (Squier)
55 US Custom Shop (Fender)
56 US Custom Shop (Fender)
57 US Custom Shop (Fender)

Model chronology

Arranged by year of first appearance. US production except where marked (J) for Japan or (M) for Mexico. Abbreviations 1st, 2nd etc indicate model version numbers.

1950
Esquire 1950-69
Broadcaster 1950-51

1951
Telecaster 1951-83

1959
Custom 1959-72
Custom Esquire 1959-69

1968
Blue Flower Telecaster 1968-69
Paisley Red Telecaster 1968-69
Thinline Telecaster 1st 1968-71

1969
Rosewood Telecaster 1969-72

1971
Thinline Telecaster 2nd 1971-79

1972
Telecaster Custom 1972-81
Telecaster Deluxe 1972-81

1977
Antigua Telecaster 1977-79
Antigua Telecaster Custom 1977-79
Antigua Telecaster Deluxe 1977-79

1981
Black & Gold Telecaster 1981-83
International Colour Telecaster 1981

1982
'52 Telecaster 1982-84, 1986-current

1983
Elite Telecaster 1983-84
Gold Elite Telecaster 1983-84
Telecaster Standard 1983-84
Walnut Elite Telecaster 1983-84

1984
'Marble' or 'Bowling Ball' Telecaster Standard 1984

1985
Contemporary Telecaster 1st (J) 1985-87
Contemporary Telecaster 2nd (J) 1985-87
Custom Telecaster '62 (J) 1985-current
Foto Flame Telecaster (J) 1995-96

1986
Esquire (J) 1986-93
Custom Esquire (J) 1986-93
Blue Flower Telecaster (J) 1986-current
Paisley Telecaster (J) 1986-current
Rosewood Telecaster (J) 1986-current
Telecaster Custom '72 (J) 1986-98
Thinline Telecaster '69 (J) 1986-98
Thinline Telecaster '72 (J) 1986-98

1988
American Standard Telecaster 1988-2000
Standard Telecaster (J) 1988-91

1990
Albert Collins Telecaster 1990-current
Danny Gatton Telecaster 1990-current
James Burton Telecaster 1990-current
Tele Plus 1st 1990-95
50s Telecaster (J) 1990-98

1991
HMT Acoustic-Electric 1st (J) 1991-94
HMT Telecaster 1st (J) 1991-92
HMT Telecaster 2nd (J) 1991-92
Set Neck Telecaster 1991-95
Set Neck Telecaster Floyd Rose 1991-92
Set Neck Telecaster Plus 1991-92
Standard Telecaster (M) 1991-current
Tele Plus Deluxe 1991-92

1992
Bajo Sexto Telecaster 1992-98
JD Telecaster (J) 1992-99
Jerry Donahue Telecaster 1992-2001
Set Neck Telecaster Country Artist 1992-95
Sparkle Telecaster 1992-95
Squier Series Standard Telecaster (K) 1992-94

1993
Clarence White Telecaster 1993-2001

1994
Aluminium-Body Telecaster 1994-95
Special Edition 1994 Telecaster 1994
Tele Special (M) 1994-96
60s Telecaster (J) 1994

1995
American Classic Telecaster 1st 1995-98
American Standard B-Bender Telecaster 1995-98
HMT Acoustic-Electric 2nd (J) 1995-97
James Burton Standard Telecaster (M) 1995-current
Relic Nocaster 1995-98
Set Neck Tele Jnr 1995-99
Tele Plus 2nd 1995-98
Telecaster XII 1995-98
Waylon Jennings Tribute Telecaster 1995-current
90s Telecaster Custom (J) 1995-97
90s Telecaster Deluxe (J) 1995-97

1996
Nokie Edwards Telecaster 1996-97
Traditional Telecaster (M) 1996-97
50th Anniversary Telecaster 1996
50s Telecaster 1996-98
60s Telecaster Custom 1996-98

1997
California Fat Tele 1997-98
California Tele 1997-98
Deluxe Nashville Tele (M) 1997-current
Merle Haggard Tele 1997-current
Tex-Mex Tele Special (M) 1997
Will Ray Jazz-A-Caster (J) 1997-98
90s Tele Thinline 1997-2000

1998
American Deluxe Telecaster 1st 1998-99
Buck Owens Telecaster (J) 1998
John Jorgenson Telecaster 1998-2001
Nashville B-Bender Tele 1998-current
Tele-Sonic 1998-2004
U.S. Fat Tele 1998-2000
Will Ray Telecaster 1998-2001
50s Telecaster (M) 1998-current
'69 Telecaster Thinline 1998-current
1998 Collectors Edition Telecaster 1998

1999
American Classic Telecaster 2nd 1999-2000
American Deluxe Telecaster 2nd 1999-2004
Closet Classic '63 Telecaster 1999-current
Deluxe Nashville Power Tele (M) 1999-current
'51 Nocaster 1999-current
'52 Tele Special 1999-2001
'62 Telecaster Custom 1999-current
'63 Telecaster 1999-current
'72 Telecaster Custom (M) 1999-current
'72 Telecaster Thinline (M) 1999-current

2000
American Deluxe Power Tele 2000-01
Custom Classic Telecaster 2000-current

2001
American Fat Tele 2001-2003
American Telecaster 2001-current
Muddy Waters Telecaster (M) 2001-current

2002
Tele Sub-Sonic 2002-current
60s Telecaster (M) 2002-current

2003
American Telecaster HH/HS 2003-current
American Telecaster 2003-current
Esquire Custom Celtic (K) 2003
Esquire Custom GT (K) 2003
Esquire Custom Scorpion (K) 2003
Highway 1 Telecaster 2003-current
J5:HB Telecaster 2003-current
J5:Bigsby 2003-current
Seymour Duncan Signature Esquire 2003-current
Telecaster Custom FMT (K) 2003-current
'59 Esquire 2003-current
'60 Telecaster Custom 2003-04

2004
Aerodyne Tele (J) 2004-current
American Ash Telecaster 2004-current
American Deluxe Telecaster 3rd 2004-current
American Deluxe Telecaster FMT/QMT 2004-current
American Deluxe Ash Telecaster 2004-current
Blackout Telecaster (K) 2004-current
Flat Head Telecaster 2004-current
Francis Rossi Signature Telecaster (J) 2004-05
Highway 1 Texas Telecaster 2004-current
Jimmy Bryant Telecaster 2004-current
Lite Ash Telecaster (K) 2004-current
Rick Parfitt Signature Telecaster (J) 2004-05
'67 Telecaster 2004-current
'72 Telecaster Deluxe (M) 2004-current

2005
John 5 Telecaster (M) 2005-current
50s Esquire (M) 2005-current
50s Telecaster With Bigsby (J) 2005-current
60s Telecaster With Bigsby (J) 2005-current

Index

Page numbers in **bold type** indicate illustrations. Page numbers in *italic type* indicate entries in the reference section.

Acknowledgements

ILLUSTRATIONS

Instrument owners
Guitars photographed came from the collections of the following individuals and organisations, and we are most grateful for their help. The owners are listed here in the alphabetical order of the code used to identify their instruments in the Key below.
AG Arbiter Group; **AH** Adrian Hornbrook; **AO** Alex Osborne; **BF** Brian Fischer; **CC** Chinery Collection; **CM** Country Music Hall Of Fame; **DG** David Gilmour; **FE** Fender Europe; **FU** Fender USA; **GR** Gruhn Guitars; **JD** Jerry Donahue; **JE** John Entwistle; **MB** Mark Brend; **PD** Paul Day; **PM** Paul Midgley; **SA** Scot Arch.

Key to instrument photographs
The following key is designed to identify who owned which guitars at the time they were photographed. After the relevant bold-type page number(s) we list the model name followed by the owner's initials (see Instrument Owners above). **14-15** Bigsby CM; **22-23** Broadcaster DG; **23** Nocaster JE; **26-27** Telecaster GR; Esquire **30-31** BF; **34** '56 Telecaster BF; **34-35** '57 Telecaster BF; **42-43** Esquire BF; **46** Custom Telecaster AH; **50-51** Telecaster SA; **54** both Telecasters BF; **58-59** Thinline Telecaster BF; **62** Telecaster BF; **62-63** Telecaster BF; **66** Paisley Red Telecaster AH; **67** B-Bender Telecaster CC; **70-71** Rosewood Telecaster AH; **71** Thinline Telecasters both BF; **74** Telecaster Deluxe PM; **74-75** Telecaster Custom BF; **78** Telecaster BF; **82-83** Telecaster BF; **86-87** Telecaster Standards all BF; **90-91** '52 Telecaster DG; **94-95** Gold Elite Telecaster PM; **95** Gold Elite Telecaster PD; **98-99** American Standard Telecaster FU; **99** Contemporary Telecaster MB, Jerry Donahue Telecaster prototype JD; **102** Egyptian Telecaster FU; **102-103** James Burton Telecaster PM, Telecaster 40th Anniversary PM; **106-107** Clarence White Telecaster FU; **107** Set Neck FU, American Classic AG, 50s Telecaster AO; **110** HMT Acoustic-Electric FU; **110-111** '63 Telecaster Relic FE; **114-115** '72 Telecaster Deluxe FE; **115** Leo Fender Broadcaster AG; **118** '59 Esquire Relic FE; **118-119** American Deluxe Telecaster FE; **119** Standard Telecaster FE.

Principal guitar photography was by William Taylor and Miki Slingsby. Other photography by Garth Blore and Matthew Chattle; some images supplied by Fender USA and Fender Europe.

Artist pictures were supplied principally by Redfern's, London. Redfern's photographers are indicated by the following key: **AW** Andrew Whittuck; **CF** Colin Fuller; **DE** David Ellis; **EE** Erica Echenberg; **EL** Elliott Landy; **EM** EMI Archives; **FC** Fin Costello; **HM** Hayley Madden; **ID** Ian Dickson **JA** Jorgen Angel;; **JD** Jill Douglas; **JF** Jeremy Fletcher; **KK** K&K Studios; **LR** Lex Van Rossen; **MG** Mick Gold; **MO** Michael Ochs Archive; **PB** Paul Bergen; **PD** Phil Dent; **PN** Petra Neimeier; **PP** Peter Pakvis; **RA** Richard E Aaron; **RP** Roberta Parkin; **SB** Sue Bradshaw; **TH** Tim Hall.

Pictures and photographers are identified by bold-type page number, subject, and the Redfern's photographer key (or, in brackets, another source). **2-3** Waters RA; **7** O'Brien PB; **18** Cooley MO, Aldrich (Richard Smith); **22** Kauffman (Richard Smith); **31** King MO; **35** Vincent (Balafon); **38** Waters MO; **46** Cropper MO; **47** Owens EM; **50** Bloomfield MO; **55** Townshend KK; **58** Clapton JF, Beck PN; **59** Barrett AW; **62** Page JA; **66** Burton SB; **70** Harrison MO; **75** Richards RA, Dias DE; **78** Rollo FC; **79** Robertson (left) EL, (right) MG, Buchanan MO; **82** Johnson CF; **83** Strummer (left) EE, (right) LR; **86** Gatton MO; **87** Summers JA; **91** Stern TH; **94** Lee PD; **95** Hynde ID; **99** Donahue RP; **106** Black PB; **111** Yorke PP; **114** Kapranos PP; **115** Ball JD; **119** Okereke HM.

MEMORABILIA illustrated in this book – including advertisements, catalogues and record sleeves – is drawn from the Balafon Image Bank. Original items came from the collections of Tony Bacon, Paul Day, *The Music Trades*, National Jazz Archive (Loughton), John Page, and Alan Rogan.

THANKS Ralph Baker; Jeff Beck; Julie Bowie; Martin Brady (Fender Europe); Mark Brend; John Bryant; Dave Burrluck; James Burton; Louise Burton; Walter Carter (Gruhn Guitars); Paul Cooper; Jerry Donahue; Mike Eldred (Fender USA); flyingvintage.com; Dave Gregory; Yvonne Groenendijk; Johnny Harper; Christopher Hjort; Bill Kirchen; John Morrish; Jun Nakabayashi (Dyna Boeki); Justin Norvell (Fender USA); John Page (p-one-c), Julian Ridgway (Redfern's); Morgan Ringwald (Fender USA); Alan Rogan; John Ryall; Dan Smith (Fender USA); Richard Smith; Simon Smith; Will Taylor; Neil Whitcher (Fender Europe); Michael Wright.

SPECIAL THANKS to Brian Fischer whose fine collection provided a good deal of the instruments pictured in this book. Thanks Brian for your help, patience, generosity and hospitality. And to Paul Day for the expertly revised reference section in this book: thank you, squier.

ORIGINAL INTERVIEWS used in this book were conducted by Tony Bacon as follows: Jeff Beck (April 2005); James Burton (April 2005); Joe Carducci (November 1997); Bill Carson (September 1991); Jerry Donahue (April 2005); Phyllis Fender (February 1992); George Fullerton (February 1992); Bob Heinrich (December 1997); Dale Hyatt (February 1992); Bill Kirchen (April 2005); Mike Lewis (December 1997); Seth Lover (October 1992); Karl Olmsted (February 1992); John Page (February 1992, December 1997); Don Randall (February 1992); Dan Smith (February 1985, February 1992, December 1997, June 2005); Andy Summers (August 1981); Forrest White (February 1992).

BOOKS

Tony Bacon *50 Years Of Fender* (Backbeat 2000)
Tony Bacon (ed) *Electric Guitars: The Illustrated Encyclopedia* (Thunder Bay 2000)
Tony Bacon & Paul Day *The Fender Book* (Balafon 1998)
Bill Carson *My Life And Times With Fender Musical Instruments* (Hal Leonard 1999)
Phil Carson *Roy Buchanan: American Axe* (Backbeat 2001)
Walter Carter & George Gruhn *Gruhn's Guide To Vintage Guitars* (Miller Freeman 1999)
A.R. Duchossoir The Fender Telecaster (Hal Leonard 1991)
George Fullerton *Guitar Legends: The Evolution Of The Guitar From Fender to G&L* (Centerstream 1993)
Hugh Gregory *1000 Great Guitarists* (Balafon 1994)
Guitar Trader *Vintage Guitar Bulletin Vol.2* (Bold Strummer 1992)
Ralph Heibutzki *Unfinished Business: The Life & Times Of Danny Gatton* (Backbeat 2003)
Christopher Hjort & Doug Hinman *Jeff's Book* (Rock'n'Roll Research Press 2000)
Steve Howe & Tony Bacon *The Steve Howe Guitar Collection* (Balafon 1994)
Richard R. Smith *Fender: The Sound Heard 'Round The World* (Garfish 1995)
Tom Wheeler *The Stratocaster Chronicles* (Hal Leonard 2004)
Forrest White *Fender: The Inside Story* (Miller Freeman 1994)

TRADEMARKS Throughout this book we have mentioned a number of registered trademark names. Rather than put a trademark or registered symbol next to every occurrence of a trademarked name, we state here that we are using the names only in an editorial fashion and that we do not intend to infringe any trademarks.

UPDATES? The author and publisher welcome any new information for future editions. Write to: Telecaster, Backbeat, 2A Union Court, 20-22 Union Road, London SW4 6JP, England. Or you can email: telecaster@backbeatuk.com.

"You can do everything on a Tele. If there's a sound you can't get, don't blame it on the axe. It means you can't pick."
DANNY GATTON, 1972